Dr Dinora Pines, one of Britain's leading pyschoanalysts, first graduated in Modern Languages, and then, following a family tradition, qualified as a Doctor of Medicine at the Royal Free Hospital, London. In addition to her engagement in general practice, she became a dermatologist in both of the London hospitals for women which existed at that time. It was this extensive clinical experience which stimulated her keen interest in the relationship of mind and body, and led her to train as a psycho-analyst at the British Society of Psychoanalysis. She is in private practice in addition to being a training analyst, supervisor and teacher at the Institute of Psychoanalysis. She continues to be invited to lecture and supervise worldwide.

For Evelyn Taylor
with best wishes
Dinora Pines

A WOMAN'S UNCONSCIOUS USE OF HER BODY

A PSYCHOANALYTICAL PERSPECTIVE

Dinora Pines

Published by VIRAGO PRESS Limited 1993
20 Vauxhall Bridge Road, London SW1V 2SA

Reprinted 1993, 1995

*A CIP catalogue record for this book is available
from the British Library*

Printed and bound in Great Britain by
Cox & Wyman Ltd, Reading, Berkshire

To my husband, my children and grandchildren,
who have been my beloved companions through my own
phases of the life cycle.

CONTENTS

ACKNOWLEDGEMENTS

I am grateful to my husband Anthony for his encouragement, to my colleague Marion Burgner who has so often been a most helpful critic and discussant, to Julia Vellacott for her sensitive editing and to Dorothy Unwin for her patient secretarial help. Above all I am grateful to the many patients who have shared their deepest feelings with me. To them I owe the ideas in this book.

INTRODUCTION

My professional life as a psychoanalyst has involved me in working with both men and women patients, sharing their deepest experiences, conscious and unconscious. Love, joy and pleasure in living both for oneself and for other people are aspects of human experience which are easily expressed. What may remain secret and unknown, in order to avoid shame and guilt, is the child's fear of abandonment, of being unlovable, the fear of loneliness, and the lifelong struggle to come to terms with one's own mortality. These anxieties are common to patient and analyst, to men and women alike, for we share a common humanity. There are, however, certain major events, such as pregnancy, that only women experience. Over time I have become especially interested in these aspects of a woman's life cycle, both from my own experience and from observing the reactions of women in my care.

1

After my early education at a girls' school, I obtained a degree in modern languages at a mixed university. By the time I was considering further studies, a war was raging that threatened England's very existence, and it felt inappropriate to begin research into medieval languages and literature. I therefore decided to study medicine, perhaps unconsciously striving to find a way of repairing, rescuing and healing human beings who were being so horribly destroyed in the outside world.

My parents were both doctors, and had always wanted me to study medicine. My arts degree was perhaps symbolic of an adolescent rebellion against them, but it was one that opened the doors to an appreciation of literature and language that has never failed to delight me. The study of great novels, with their intense human relationships and feelings, formed an appropriate foundation for the close study of feelings and relationships that every patient brings to the consulting room. Sensitive listening to language, the choice of words and their meaning, is as important in psychoanalysis as in literature.

During the war, in 1940, very few medical schools accepted women. So I enrolled at the London School of Medicine for Women, where clinical studies were conducted at the Royal Free Hospital. All the students were women, as were most of the staff, since the men were in the forces. Air raids were frequent. A V-2 destroyed the casualty department just after we students on duty had left. After that we became evacuees, unwelcome guests of the families with whom we were billeted and a long way from our own families, from whom we were frequently cut off as telephone lines came down. Very early on in our lives we experienced in reality the powerful forces of life and death, our own vulnerability and that of those around us. Of course this was as nothing compared with the rest of Europe, whose countries were invaded, many of their citizens imprisoned or murdered for racial or political reasons.

On our qualification in 1945 most of us were eager to take an active part in the war, but by then there were enough doctors in the forces and we were deployed to various hospitals where we cared for the civilian population. By this time rumours had begun to emerge as to what had taken place in the concentration camps. I was secretly recruited to head a relief team that would be sent to Auschwitz, but mysteriously, the group was disbanded and no reason was ever given. It was a great disappointment to me, as by then I suspected that members of my family whom I had known as a child had been murdered. My interest in the Holocaust at that time stood me in good stead when I later began to work with victims of those years.

When I began clinical practice as a doctor, I gradually learnt to listen very carefully to what my patients were telling me or – even more important – not telling me as I examined their bodies. The relationship between body and mind impressed itself more and more on me through my work. I have described in my paper 'Skin Communication' (see Chapter 1 below) how vividly the women patients' bodies expressed pain that was unbearable and unthinkable about. Because words were unavailable to them, their emotions had to be expressed somatically and understood by a woman doctor who could *think* about each patient's predicament as if she were a mother, and try to bring relief. In this way the phenomena of transference and countertransference between patient and doctor began to impinge upon my medical training, and made me seek to understand more. I was very fortunate in meeting a colleague in my own hospital, Hilda Abraham, who was an analyst – the daughter of Karl Abraham, one

3

of the first disciples of Sigmund Freud. She encouraged me to discuss my cases with her and to try to work on similar analytic lines. The insights she gave me were my first experience of the existence and power of the unconscious. None of this knowledge was at that time part of our medical studies. Fortunately, this is no longer the case.

For a time I went into general practice, and saw even more aspects of men's and women's lives. Adolescent girls experiencing the inevitable bodily changes of puberty and the emotional impact of powerful sexual urges could either accept such changes in their bodies, or deny the move to adult femininity by becoming amenorrhoeic or anorexic, thereby avoiding the secondary sexual characteristics of an adult feminine body, such as breasts. Young women marrying, becoming pregnant, giving birth to babies and mothering them, expressed their joy, but also their emotional difficulties. They could be heard and helped by an attentive practitioner who saw them in their own homes, knew their husbands and their mothers and their other children. Husbands, and their problems in becoming fathers and heads of families, were another part of the picture. Thus the family crisis that inevitably follows the birth of a new baby could be observed in reality by the doctor rather than seen through the eyes of the mother alone.

When I trained as a psychoanalyst between 1959 and 1964 and began to practise, these same problems appeared in the patient's narrative, but my deeper understanding of myself gained through my own analysis now enabled me to listen better, to try to understand the patient's pain and enter into a psychoanalytic dialogue. Part of this dialogue consisted of listening to what the patient was *not* saying, and noting how the body was forced to act out feelings that could not be consciously

4

known or transmitted. I saw that many patients somatized rather than spoke. They would frequently develop a transient rash at moments of stress, or abdominal pains would interrupt their narrative at a point where painful feelings might otherwise have to be acknowledged. In several patients with a history of asthma, feelings of aggression expressed in the transference were accompanied by loud wheezing in their breathing, though a full asthmatic attack was avoided by verbalization and making the unconscious conscious in the session.

It seemed to me that these bodily expressions of unbearable feelings were more common in women patients. In thinking about this observation I came to realize that a mature woman's body offers her a means of avoiding conscious thought and facing psychic conflict. For example, my patients gradually taught me to be sensitive to the uses and abuses of pregnancy. Consciously a woman might become pregnant in order to have a baby, but unconsciously her ambivalence to her pregnancy might be acted out in miscarriage or abortion. Pregnancy may also be used to solve unconscious conflicts concerning sexual identity, or other psychic difficulties such as unconscious rage against the mother.

Even if a woman does not use her body to avoid the knowledge of conflict, she is nevertheless deeply influenced by bodily changes throughout life, and different women cope with these events in line with their own ability to manage life problems and their own previous histories. The finality of the ending of the child-bearing years is frequently accompanied by the painful death of so many fantasied future babies in a woman's mind, babies who will never now be conceived and born in reality. The pain of remaining barren when all around her are fertile is devastating and difficult to bear. A woman's ageing body and the loss of her fertility may be a severe blow to her self-esteem, as if it were the death of a part of herself that was attractive to men. Yet it may force her to find a new solution to her life, and new areas of living once the mourning for this part of her life cycle has been achieved.

Finally, I have been privileged to work with victims of the Holocaust and bear witness to some of their impressive ability to live their lives again after such massive traumatization, creating new life in themselves and in others. None the less, secrets about their past may be retained in their analyses, and in their families in a way which affects the next generation. Others are not so fortunate – despite the analyst's strong wish to rescue them from somatizing unbearable emotional pain, they remain victims. Yet I am convinced that for all the patients I have worked with and described in this book, making the unconscious conscious in psychoanalysis leads to new and enriched life – secrets that are revealed allow room for the patient to *think* rather than to act out.

This collection of papers, written over the past twenty years, describes my psychoanalytic journey and some of the problems that I hope I have understood more clearly over time. Reading them over has made me aware of my own increasing emphasis on the importance of benevolent and compassionate listening, no matter what the analyst's theoretical orientation. Such a stance is sometimes difficult to maintain in a psychoanalytic dialogue, as it is in any close relationship between two people where one's own feelings of hatred and destructiveness towards the other may be unconsciously aroused, however strongly they are consciously defended against. For the analyst is human, not ideal. Benevolence does not imply that the analyst's use of critical thought is suspended, but that the patient experiences in the psychoanalytic dialogue an atmosphere of compassion which enables him or her to expose the angry, hurt child inside and re-examine past solutions without shame.* In my view the past cannot be erased, but a more mature understanding of oneself and others may help to replace rage with compassion, and thus enable the patient to seize the opportunity for a new beginning and a greater pleasure in living.

Much still remains to be understood, not only by me but by others working in the field – I look forward to learning from them now and in the future. I am grateful to my patients who have shared the analytic experience with me and taught me to understand more than I understood at the beginning.

Note

* To avoid the ungainliness of writing 'he or she' when referring to a psychoanalyst and to a patient, since this book is by a female analyst and is focused upon the problems of women patients, I have used the feminine gender only.

SKIN COMMUNICATION:

Early Skin Disorders and Their Effect on Transference and Countertransference*

Introduction

In this paper I shall describe and discuss the psychic predicament of female patients who have suffered from infantile eczema during the first year of life. After drawing on direct observations from my previous experience as a consultant dermatologist in a women's hospital, I shall discuss the analysis of a patient with a history of this disease. I will concentrate on transference–countertransference problems, since in my view they highlight a basic disturbance in the earliest mother–infant relationship. This disturbance is renewed with every

---

* Presented at the 31st International Psychoanalytical Congress, New York, August 1979. Published in *International Journal of Psycho-Analysis* (1980) 61: 315–22.

transitional phase of the life cycle, and exerts a subtle influence upon it.

The Skin as a Means of Communication

I am focusing on the fundamental importance of the skin as a means of communication between mother and infant while she provides the holding environment, in which primary identification of the self is founded. In Leboyer's (1974) film of the process of birth, we observe the immediate soothing effect of skin-to-skin contact between neonate and mother after the infant has abruptly emerged from the mother's warm body into a cold and non-containing world.

Skin contact re-establishes the mother's intimate feelings for her baby, as if they were once again merged, like they were in pregnancy, when the mother's skin contained them both. The skin becomes a medium for physical contact, for the comfort of holding and of being held, and also for the transmission of smell, touch, taste and warmth, sensations which can be a source of pleasure and intimacy to mother and infant alike. The skin establishes the boundary of self and non-self, and represents the container of the self for each one of them. It is one of their most primitive channels for preverbal communication, where non-verbalized affects may be somatically experienced and observed.

Through her handling of the child the mother's skin may convey the full range of emotions, from tenderness and warmth and love to disgust and hate.

The infant may react through its skin to the mother's positive feelings by a sense of well-being, and to her negative feelings by a skin disorder, which can take varying forms. The child's non-verbalized affects may find expression through the skin. The skin may itch, the skin may weep, and the skin may rage. It will be dealt with by the mother according to her capacity to accept and soothe her blemished child. Such a situation may be internalized by the infant, as Bick's (1968) paper has described. She shows how the containing object, the mother, is experienced concretely as a skin, and that her capacity to contain the infant's anxiety is introjected by the infant. This function gives rise to the notion of internal and external space. Failure to introject the containing function and to accept the containment of self and object in separate skins leads to pseudo-independence, and to 'adhesive identification' and inability to recognize the separate existence of self and object.

Direct Observation in the Hospital Setting

As a young dermatologist in a busy hospital, I observed that some patients with extensive skin disorders, who did not respond to medical treatment alone, would often be helped by my untrained attempts at therapy combined with sympathy and appropriate ointments. I noticed that some would lose their symptomatology, while others would improve but relapse when my holiday interrupted our relationship. Despite my own reaction of shock to the sadistic attacks some women made upon their bodies by tearing at their skins, or my revulsion at their appearance, I retained a feeling of pity and empathy for their obvious suffering and a wish to relieve their affliction.

Some patients reacted to my pregnancy by leaving other consultants and attaching themselves to me. Their observation of my condition was as silent as the pain which lay behind the skin disorder. When I returned from maternity leave, they enquired, and they were obviously relieved to hear that all was well. They seemed to relive their life history vicariously by watching me in mine and felt that, with my new experience, I could now truly begin to understand them. After some time, they gradually spoke of the intolerable experiences of object loss and uncompleted mourning which had been expressed through the raging or weeping skin.

Mrs A, an elderly widow, was covered with a raw, seeping rash. She gave a previous history of infantile eczema. Her appearance disturbed me, as did her silence, although her face was set in a rigid mask of pain. Nevertheless, I talked to her, and dressed her skin myself. When I returned from maternity leave, the rash gradually receded. Later Mrs A could tell me that the rash recurred only as she put the key in her front door on Fridays and subsided when she went back to work on Mondays. When I asked her if anything had happened in the hall, she told me that when she entered the house one Friday she had found her son's body hanging there. As a new mother I too was shocked and silenced. Having given me her feelings to hold, Mrs A could weep for the first time as she recalled that terrible memory and mourned her son. Her rash disappeared soon after. My psychoanalytic training has since helped me to understand that she had to shock me with her body, as her son had shocked her by his.

Psychoanalytic Understanding of Direct Observation

Freud (1905, 1912), describing transference phenomena, stressed that transference was highlighted by the analytic situation but that it existed in every doctor–patient relationship. The therapeutic alliance created could then be used to enable the patient to accomplish a psychic task that effected cure. Winnicott (1965) emphasized the important role of the maturational environment provided by the mother in the primitive stages of ego development. This was reflected in the importance of both analyst and analytic setting in the establishment of the therapeutic alliance. Many writers – including M. Balint (1950, 1952), Khan (1974) and James (1978) – have elaborated this aspect and extended our understanding.

The writings of Heimann (1950, 1956), Hoffer (1956) and King (1978) have alerted the analyst to the importance of acknowledging her response to her patient. King (1978) has in particular emphasized the need for the analyst to be particularly sensitive to her own countertransference feelings in the analysis of patients where the preverbal trauma was not only due to the infant's own condition but was also contributed to by the mother's affective response to it.

The hospital setting could then be seen as representing the primitive holding environment, where transference–countertransference feelings could be experienced by patient and doctor alike. The patient sought help where she could repeatedly be a child again and let another woman touch her and soothe her pain. Preverbal communication and physical contact could bring relief and hope of cure when verbal communication was blocked. In my view these patients avoid hopeless despair by finding a psychosomatic solution to psychic pain. They can safely regress and regain the most primitive form of maternal comfort. In this way they repeat their infantile experience of a mother who can care for the body but not the feelings.

The Psychoanalytic Situation

The psychoanalytic situation as described by Limentani (1977) reproduces the early mother–child relationship, but with the basic difference that physical contact is not available. This limitation is a particular frustration to patients who, whether they know it or not, have had a history of infantile eczema. Such patients may have found a maternal figure to soothe their body, but they have not been able to separate from her at the appropriate time. Hallucination and fantasy, or the use of a transitional object, are unsatisfactory and unsatisfying, since the infant's sole source of soothing and tranquillity is the mother, and the balm that she applies. Mothers of these children may be faced with the impossible task of constantly soothing a fretful, restless baby. Their function as a protective shield for the child (Khan, 1963) may then be impaired, since the child's demands may exceed the patient care that even the good-enough mother can provide. These babies not only suffer the physical discomfort of a damaged skin, but are particularly vulnerable to overwhelming feelings of uncontained primitive aggression. They are also deprived of an adequate maternal mirroring response of admiration and love for the child's body. The mother's narcissistic disappointment in her infant's appearance will be reflected in her response to its demands, and will have a fundamental effect upon the child's own narcissistic structure and self-representation.

E. Balint (1973), discussing technical difficulties in the analysis of women patients by a woman analyst, focuses on the little girl's introjection and identification with a satisfactory and satisfying woman's body. This occurs only if she has satisfied and been satisfied bodily by her mother. The patients whom I am describing have never internalized a primary stable satisfying basis of well-being, since their bodily experience with their mothers has been both satisfying and unsatisfying in the original situation of the nursing couple. The little girl who has felt that she has not satisfied her mother bodily at this stage, nor been adequately satisfied by her, can never make up

13

for this basic loss. For unless she sacrifices her normal drive towards a positive oedipal outcome, as well as her move towards a mature female identity, she can never physically satisfy her mother again.

The patient enters the analytic situation with the hope of being understood, and encountered truly by the analyst. Yet from the outset the patients whom I describe are also haunted by the opposing fear of re-experiencing that primary narcissistic hurt, the shame of the blemished and exposed infant. They are, in my experience, unusually sensitive and observant, suffering from pervasive anxiety which may lead to borderline symptomatology. They perceive the minutest alteration in the analyst's mood, tone of voice, and appearance, and are easily over-whelmed by the fear of their own aggression. They placate, imitate and please the analyst to the detriment of their own psychic health. They secretly long to repeat their unduly prolonged primary experience of the unity of mother and baby, with its psychic containment and physical soothing. Yet the emotional encounter with the analyst arouses great anxiety. There is a strong wish to merge with the object but also an intense fear of regression and loss of the self.

A disturbance in concepts of the self, linked with narcissistic difficulties and acute sensitivity to object relationships, may be anticipated in the analysis of such patients, and prove to be a difficulty for patient and analyst alike.

The character of the transference is determined by the patient's capacity to contain feelings, to define personal identity and to defend against fear of total annihilation. Kohut describes patients who show a lack of internalized structure, and use the analyst as a direct continuation of an early interpersonal object reality.[1] The transference in the patient described in this paper also resembles the 'addictive transference' described by McDougall (1974), in which the analyst becomes the centre of the patient's life, re-creating the self-object of the mother–infant relationship and obscuring all others. Separation from the analyst is dealt with not by normal mourning or grief, but by means of a psychosomatic event or a transient psychosis.

In the second type of transference the patient appears to have a more secure sense of self, to have achieved more independence from the mother in the separation–individuation phase, entered the oedipal phase, and resolved it to some degree. The patient may, therefore, present a comparatively normal life history and character formation. Nevertheless the same intense anxieties about attachment and ambivalence towards the mother may be reactivated in the transference to a female analyst, which the patient may attempt to escape by means of acting out or somatization of primitive and overwhelming affects.

A split in the patient's ego, Winnicott's 'False Self',[2] frequently occurs, in order to avoid experiencing the shame and narcissistic pain resulting from total exposure. While clinging to the analyst, there is a parallel wish to be rid of the analyst's intrusion into a private world, and the clues the patient gives are very muddled. Such patients are often as sensitive to the analyst's unconscious countertransference as they once were to the mother's ambivalence and capacity or incapacity to mother them. It follows that the countertransference is one that puts a strain on the analyst. The patient's transference, which was such a positive factor in the hospital setting, now becomes an analytic problem. The regressive longing to be held and soothed by the mother/analyst is directly counterbalanced by the intense anxiety aroused by emotional closeness. Fear of merging and loss of self is a constant threat.

Clinical Material
First phase of the analysis

Mrs B had her first analysis following a severe depression with suicidal and psychotic episodes. Hypochondriacal fears had affected her whole life, but by the end of her analysis she had become an attractive woman who functioned well within her immediate family. Occasional telephone contact with her analyst maintained her, until he emigrated. Then she became so depressed and unable to verbalize it even to herself that she engineered a road accident in which she received multiple skin injuries. Admitted to hospital, she regressed so much that she would eat only if fed by the psychiatrist, and refused to get out of bed. There she developed a profuse rash, in this way expressing the despair and anger that she could not verbalize. When she was referred to me, Mrs B, in spite of her obvious depression and confusion, was always neatly dressed, and began her first session by asking me what I thought was appropriate Hampstead analytic gear, as if to say, 'What disguise shall I put on to please you and hide my real self with?'

This theme of sensitively attempting to give me not only the outward appearance she thought I wanted, but also the feeling that she thought I wanted her to feel, continued throughout the analysis. My analytic role – and I often failed in it – was to try to help her to get in touch with her true feelings. They had been split off so early that she could no longer reach them. Mrs B's intense suicidal feelings were relieved by frequent frantic telephone calls to me for instant attention, as if she were a baby who could be calmed only by the soothing sound of a voice which could hold her fear of disintegration. She neglected her family. Yet no matter how confused and frightened she felt, Mrs B, between sessions with me, meticulously oiled her skin after her daily bath, and put herself to bed for a nap. These were rituals that she had always performed since her nanny had begun them.

The first phase of her second analysis was a testing time for us both. We each needed to test not only my ability to hold her, but also my capacity to recognize and contain the aggressive feelings experienced in the counter-transference, in response to her 'irritating and scratching transference'. My countertransference was intense. I felt confused, muddled, and at times almost mad. Mrs B was compliant, punctual, but her dreams and associations made no sense, nor could I recall them clearly. Yet despite the incessant phone calls, and my own worry and confusion, I felt deeply concerned and wished to help. When Mrs B told me that her favourite prank was to mislead tourists about the buildings which they were looking at, I understood that she was testing my capacity to tolerate confusion. Mrs B was also showing me her own, which had existed since the beginning of her life. No true feelings of her own had been acknowledged or confirmed by her mother, although her body had been conscientiously cared for by the nanny. So caretaking had been inconsistently both good and bad and, therefore, muddling to the growing child. Yet Mrs B was in daily contact with her mother, who could still confuse her. Mrs B felt cared for by her only when she was physically or mentally ill. This had been the secondary gain throughout her life, and was a threat to the therapeutic alliance. To get well was to risk losing her mother's care for the sick child. We understood that Mrs B's past psychic health had been founded on a clever limitation of her previous therapist, and on compliance with what she thought he wanted. Following his loss, what had appeared to be depression or mourning was in fact a total loss of the self, since the self-object had now disappeared, and the imitation of the

17

analyst could not be maintained. Mrs B regressed to the only condition that felt real to her, that of being the special ill child.

Joseph's (1975) paper stresses how the pseudo-co-operative part of the patient prevents the really needy part from getting into contact with the analyst, and that if we are taken in by this we cannot expect a change in our patients, because we do not make contact with the part that needs the experience of being understood, as opposed to getting understanding. Mrs B was extremely observant, and able to pick up any fluctuation in my countertransference, or in my attentive listening. Yet I was also impressed by her massive denial of any fatigue or sadness in me. She could not contain any frailty of mine, for she was always the infant in the nursing couple. As Mrs B became less depressed, my quietness and different interpretive style from that of her previous therapist became a source of anxiety. It was not until I realized how many cues I was still giving her that we began to work on her imitation of me and her compliance.

Second phase of the analysis

Mrs B related that she had been the youngest child, and that shortly after her birth her father had gone into the army. Her childhood was miserable, and she felt a misfit, both in her family and at school. Mrs B was withdrawn, apathetic and lonely, but inside the suffering child there was a talent for observation, criticism and mimicry, which was occasionally encouraged by her father. These few positive experiences were sources of intense pleasure to her, but the talent had to be hidden from her critical mother, just as it could never be displayed to me. Both at home and in her analysis, she always presented herself as hopeless and helpless.

18

For years Mrs B's feelings of elation had been labelled manic and her down days depressive, although she herself saw them as normal wide-ranging mood-swings. She had complained of paralysing tiredness to her doctors, who attributed it to her depression, although she believed in a physical cause. I suspected a thyroid dysfunction, and this was confirmed by a female consultant who prescribed treatment for her. Mrs B began to feel physically better, and a different analytic atmosphere ensued. The validity of Mrs B's own perception of her body dysfunction had been sympathetically acknowledged by two women, mother and nanny in the transference. Now she felt she could allow herself to show her true feeling states, and a manic triumph followed.

This was the moment at which the first encounter with Mrs B's fiercely guarded real self appeared in the analysis. Her compliance, both in the analysis and at home, vanished. Now she expressed fury with me at the least sign of my not having understood her, or of relaxing my attentive mood. She screamed loudly or physically attacked the couch, as if she were attacking me. Her hands swelled up and irritated her. At times she wore gloves over them. These outbursts frightened us both, but later, as we learnt to survive them, Mrs B found relief from having expressed long-repressed affects. She not only felt grateful to her husband for standing by her in her illness, but also raged at him, and physically attacked him for old narcissistic wounds which she had never admitted even to herself. Mrs B became worryingly anorexic, and we understood later that this was her declaration of independence. She no longer imitated me, whom she saw as maternal, plump, and feeding myself and others. Mrs B began to telephone the referring psychiatrist when she panicked, and was infuriated when he referred her back to me. It was as if she had for the first time encountered the parental couple who could not be omnipotently divided. When her father went to war, Mrs B's fantasy was that her birth had divided her parents. My own countertransference altered dramatically. Unusually, I became angry and actively disliked my patient for making me feel and look helpless, and incompetent. I felt in a muddle again. Was she introjecting my hate, or was she projecting hers on to me? Once I understood that I hated Mrs B because she wanted me to, and that she was facing her own hatred of me without regressing into being the ill child, the analytic atmosphere shifted. It became clear that she was growing up in the analysis and testing that hate could be survived without total destruction of either of us.

Mrs B then brought several dreams in which she was dressed up as a man. Although the acting-out and the dreaming appeared to indicate that the dyadic situation in the analysis had developed into a triangular oedipal one, this was as false as it had been in her life history. Her longing for her absent father was resolved in the dreams by assuming his outward appearance. These dreams and fantasies expressed her feeling that the only way of pleasing me, the mother analyst, with her body, was to dress like a man and excite me as her mother had been excited by her father when he returned from the war. All Mrs B's relationships were repetitions of the nursing couple. Her father had been physically absent during her infancy and psychically absent when he returned. Both the male analyst and her husband had been maternal figures in her psychic life, but she spared them the primitive hatred and rage evoked by her helpless dependence on them, just as she had primarily withheld them from her mother. Explosion was avoided by regression and loss of ego boundaries, or by compliance. Her second analysis, this time with a female who could physically be a mother, seemed to provide a new dimension for psychic growth.

Third phase of the analysis

After we had worked through this material, Mrs B's anger and irritation began to be sublimated into mimicry of me, which could at times be sadistic and cruel. She was amazed that I could survive this onslaught of hate and envy, just as she was amazed that her marriage could survive it. For the first time in her life Mrs B had let another person experience her split-off rage. She now allowed herself to expose both a shameful body image, and a despair of ever pleasing her mother or herself with her appearance. She told me that as an adolescent she had had acne and severe facial hair, and that as a young child she had worn an eye-patch to correct a squint, and a brace to correct her teeth. Mrs B remembered consciously deciding then to accept her ugly, smelly self and never expose it to anyone. After that, she kept her shameful body hidden, physically and psychically, even from her first analyst. She said, 'How can you tell a man all this? I feel as if you are removing layer after layer of make-up and skin away from me, and I'm no longer embarrassed or ashamed.'

Following this session, Mrs B dreamt that her body was covered with a profuse rash. The next day her body was red and itchy. She now learned from her mother that she had had infantile eczema as a baby, and that her mother, not her nanny, had applied the soothing creams. This was the archaic relationship that Mrs B was always striving to regain, although she did not remember it. As she grew older, her mother massively denied her own disappointment as well as her daughter's distress. The child recognized her mother's disapproval and her hidden disappointment that constant visits to doctors did little to improve her appearance. Her mother repeatedly told her how lucky she was. She could get help from doctors, she had enough food and a roof over her head. Her mother said that she was sent to a good boarding school because her parents loved her. How could she possibly be unhappy!

Mrs B *knew* she was deeply miserable and had given up ever trying to express her true feelings to anyone, even to herself. As an adult, the ugly, smelly, dirty child, as she had remained in her self-representation, was hidden behind an elegant façade, as were the narcissistic rage and hatred of her mother. It was only in the course of her second analysis that she could reconstruct from her dreams that she had had an early experience of soothing bodily care from her mother, and not from her nanny. Since the mother could not provide sufficient emotional care for her child, Mrs B's capacity to bear psychic pain was limited, for she had not internalized comforting parents. Psychically she chose to remain the dependent infant who should be mothered, and thus sacrificed much of her individuation.

Conclusion

I have drawn upon material taken from observation of women with skin diseases, and from the analysis of a woman with a history of infantile eczema. The eczematous patient had a prolonged experience of physical soothing by her mother, and the symbiotic phase was unduly extended. My first aim has been to show that the preverbal trauma of infantile eczema results not only in a fundamental disturbance of the mother–infant relationship, but also in repeated unconscious attempts to regain contact with the archaic object which had provided a primitive experience of being bodily soothed. The longing appears to persist throughout the life cycle, and is interwoven with every new relationship. The patient's hope of integrating that object, and its comforting role with the self, is repeatedly revived, but then withdrawn. Primitive fear of loss of the self is a powerful threat to individuation.

Secondly, I have tried to show that the mother's human disappointment in her baby's appearance gives rise to a basic narcissistic hurt, which the reality successes of adult life may do little to soothe. The early self-image persists and remains unaltered in the true self. Despite the enriching reality of a long relationship with a man, the profound emotional maturation established by the birth of a child, and the rearing of normal children, there may remain the painful gap in the early relationship with the mother, which is re-experienced at each transitional stage of the life cycle.

These patients, adapting to their mothers' inability to contain their emotional distress, and having had such extended periods of bodily soothing, find an alternative means of communication. They learn to translate psychic pain into visible bodily suffering, and so arouse concern and care again. In this way they learn to bypass the psychic process of suffering intolerable pain. It follows that the physical treatment of women patients by women doctors, in the hospital setting, re-enacts the most primitive and soothing contact of mother and baby.

The analytic setting, with its absence of physical contact, is a particular frustration to these patients. Their narcissistic difficulties, linked with a disturbance in concepts of the self, and their extreme sensitivity to object relationships, make both transference and countertransference feelings difficult to endure. The patient's transference highlights the regressive longing to be held and soothed, together with an opposing strong fear of

23

emotional closeness, since primitive anxieties about merging and loss of the self are equally revived. Children whose infantile eczema had repulsed their mothers suffer intense shame, and later may regard the analysis as a potential situation where shame may be re-experienced. It follows that the analyst may be perceived not only as a containing skin protecting them from disintegration but also as an intruder into a painful inner world. A split in the ego protects the patient's true feelings from psychic exposure even to herself, and compliance and imitation may be substituted for them. Nevertheless, the transference feelings remain intense and the patient may resort to acting-out in order to escape.

The countertransference feelings may be equally strong. These patients test the analyst's capacity for containing not only the patient's projection of primitive aggressive feelings but also the irritation aroused in the analyst. They may be demanding and intrusive with little capacity to contain themselves, or to care for the object that soothes them. It is as if they must always remain the infant in the dyadic situation. A woman analyst's physical capacity to be a mother appears to facilitate the transference of primitive feelings arising from partial maternal deprivation. Such patients demand much tolerance from the analyst, but also arouse a wish to relieve and soothe their pain. They are tiring, since their keen observation and unusual sensitivity to the analyst necessitate an equally sensitive monitoring of countertransference feelings. Such patients are challenging, since they evoke anxiety and confusion in the analyst, unless the primitive nature of the disturbance is picked up in the subtle interaction of the analytic situation. Once the therapeutic alliance has been tested, these patients can eventually accomplish the psychic task of experiencing Winnicott's 'primitive agony'. Verbalization of long-repressed affects, such as intense rage and anger, may be facilitated, and regression and somatization given up. Nevertheless, the psychic pain of these patients is very real, as is their hope of being found and understood by the analyst, so that a new beginning, with true individuation and separation, can be made.

Notes

1. 'an unstructured psyche struggling to maintain contact with an archaic object or to keep up the tenuous separation from it. Here the analyst is not the screen for the projection of internal structure (transference), but the direct continuation of an early reality that was too distant, too rejecting, or too unreliable to be transformed into solid psychological structures' (Kohut, 1959, pp. 470–71).

2. Winnicott (1965) describes the split in the ego that may arise when the mother's adaptation to the infant is not good enough at the start: 'The False Self has one positive and very important function: to hide the True Self, which it does by compliance with environmental demands. In the extreme examples of False Self development, the True Self is so well hidden that spontaneity is not a feature in the infant's living experiences. Compliance is then the main feature with imitation as a speciality.' He goes on: 'The False Self is a defence against that which is unthinkable, the exploitation of the True Self which would result in its annihilation' (p. 147).

THE PSYCHOANALYTIC DIALOGUE:
Transference and Countertransference*

I n the British Psycho-Analytical Society today, analysts emphasize – both in their own clinical practice and in teaching – the importance of the observation, understanding and interpretation of transference and countertransference phenomena – that is to say, the careful monitoring of the emotional and affective relationship between the two people engaged in the process of psychoanalysis: the analyst and the analysand. Both are engaged with each other in an intense ongoing human relationship to which they have each brought their previous life experiences, their conscious and unconscious feelings, wishes and desires, as well as their current life situations outside the analytic space. It could be said that this is true of any two people who enter into a close and

* Paper in the series Psychoanalysis in Britain, 1984–1989, given annually at the British Psycho-Analytical Society.

regular relationship. However, the special framework of the analytic space, the conditions imposed by the analyst in order to facilitate the therapeutic working-through of the patient's problems, make the analytic relationship a very special one. The analyst invites the patient to enter into an intense and intimate relationship, yet at the same time imposes the frustrations of the absence of normal bodily contact, bodily communication, and bodily gratification. She invites the patient to expose herself, yet at the same time hides herself as much as possible in order to facilitate the emergence of the patient's feelings about important figures of the past and present which are projected on to the analyst. These are experienced as almost real in the transference.

Freud (1912) remarked that the analytic process does not create transference but reveals it. Thus, in our daily work, both analyst and patient deal with the most powerful human passions in an intense way. The uneasy compromises that each human being must make between her own interests and those of the other are frequently tested. The healthy strivings of each child to grow into a separate individual, to obtain the sexual freedom that attends physical and psychic maturation and to come down on the positive side of ambivalence, are countered by powerful pulls towards the safety of regression, inability to separate from the original objects and hatred of them for their imprisonment, whether fantasied or real. Today we acknowledge that the conflicts of the child and the adolescent in the adult, and their affective responses, are easily mobilized in analyst and patient alike, for we now see analysis as a two-person two-way process, although Freud did not view it as such. Analyst and patient share a common humanity and a common developmental path.

Thus the topic I am describing and discussing here has arisen out of the clinical practice of psychoanalysis. If we now regard psychoanalysis as a relationship between two people, it becomes very difficult to define precisely, since each analyst and each analysand will experience transference and countertransference in their individual ways.

To begin at the beginning. In his *Autobiographical Study* (1935) Freud wrote:

Transference is a universal phenomenon of the human mind and it in fact dominates the whole of each person's relationships to his human environment.

In 1895 he had already noted transference phenomena, which he viewed as a source of *resistance* to the analytic process, and in 1909 he pointed out:

Transference arises spontaneously in all human relationships just as it does between the patient and the physician.

At that time Freud was defining transference as the patient's direct allusions to the person of the analyst and recognizing the readily defined displacements on to the analyst.

As clinical experience increased, many analysts began to regard transference as the most valuable means of understanding the patient's psychic reality, rather than the original resistance that Freud had understood it to be. Later analysts developed wider definitions of transference. Greenson, writing in 1965, said:

Transference is the experiencing of feelings, drives, attitudes, fantasies and defences towards a person in the present which are inappropriate to that person and are a repetition and displacement of reactions originating in relation to significant persons of early childhood.

He went on to emphasize that for a reaction to be considered transference it must be a repetition of the past and it must be inappropriate to the present. Willi Hoffer (1956), a distinguished training analyst of the British Society, wrote in 1956 that the term transference stresses an aspect of the influence our childhood has on our life as a whole. It thus refers to those observations in which people, in their contact with objects – which may be real or imaginary, positive, negative or ambivalent – transfer their *memories* of significant previous experiences and thus change the reality of their objects, invest them with qualities from the past, judge them and try to make use of them in accordance with their own past. Greenson, Hoffer, and many other analysts, notably Phyllis Green-acre (1954), thus stress the importance of the infantile experience derived essentially from the foundation of the mother–child relationship.

Psychoanalytic interest and research have now broad-ened our view of the complexities of human development. Although, indubitably, the past must influence the present and the future, many analysts now recognize the import-ance of the psychic changes involved at each of the maturational stages of the life cycle beyond childhood, such as adolescence, parenthood and old age. These understandings have also widened our understanding of transference. For during an analytic session the patient, in the relationship with the analyst, may relive infantile feelings and affects which are linked with the object relationships of childhood. In the same session she may switch to a later stage of development and re-experience feelings, affects and object relationships from adolescence, and the analyst must carefully monitor the changes that invariably occur during the course of the hour.

The broadening use of the transference leads many analysts to interpret anything the patient may say or do during the course of the hour as a purely transference manifestation. That is to say, the patient's material conveys a conscious or unconscious revival in the present of the patient's infantile past and its affective components. I do not adhere to this broadened view myself, for it may place the person of the analyst beyond the reality-testing of the patient, and obstruct the analyst's need for self-scrutiny and observation. We must bear in mind that the patient, as an accurate observer of her analyst, may well observe changes of mood and feelings; and naturally, reality situations which change daily must also influence the course of the session. We are all familiar with the patient who uses projection and externalization as a defence. On entering the room she may say, 'You look very stern today. You haven't smiled', whereas the analyst will recognize this as a projection of the patient's own emotional state, since she feels quite cheerful. In my view, however, if the patient has accurately perceived that the analyst is in a subdued or painful state of mind, it is important for the analyst carefully to acknowledge the reality of this, since otherwise it may reinforce the patient's infantile situation of not trusting her own feelings and perceptions of her parents. In my view the analyst's acknowledgement of the patient's perceptions is a less mechanistic procedure than that of interpreting only the patient's projections on to the analyst, or interpreting the analyst's view that the patient has used the analyst as a container for her own unbearable feelings. A human container, whether it be the analyst or the parent, is never neutral, and it is part of the analyst's search for reality to acknowledge her own projections.

I now wish to turn to the topic of countertransference – that is, the analyst's monitoring and acknowledgement of her own unconscious affective reaction to her patient and her communications. We might say that for most analysts of the British Society, the use of countertransference has become one of the major technical shifts in the practice of analysis today. Freud had declared in 1912 that the analyst should behave:

> as the surgeon who puts aside all his own feelings, including that of human sympathy, and concentrates his mind on one single purpose, that of performing the operation as skilfully as possible.

In the past, many analysts regarded their emotional response to their patients as a pathological phenomenon to be resisted rather than a valuable aspect of the analytic relationship, facilitating further understanding of the patient.

A training analyst of the British Society, Paula Heimann (1950), drew attention in a seminal paper to the positive aspects of the analyst's use of her countertransference:

> My thesis is that the analyst's emotional response to his patient within the analytic situation represents one of the most important tools for his work.

She postulated that to regard all perception of feelings in the analyst as neurotic or poor technique deprives the analyst of an important source of information, particularly that relating to the patient's preverbal experiences.

This work has been followed and elaborated by other analysts of the British Society, notably in 1978 by Pearl King. She reviewed the analyst's affective response to the patient's communications:

> [A] true understanding of transference phenomena includes not only the knowledge of who or what the analyst is representing but also what are the affects that a person or object from the past are felt by the

patient to have had towards the patient as well as those affects that the patient had towards the significant figures from the past, especially during his infancy and early childhood.

She goes on to stress the importance of the analyst defining for herself what aspect of her parents the patient is re-experiencing in the transference at that moment, and transferring on to the analyst. Is it, for example, a depressed mother or a loving one that she re-experiences during the analytic hour? She further stresses the importance of distinguishing between countertransference as a pathological phenomenon, as I delineated above, and the analyst's affective response to the patient's communications and to the various forms the patient's transference takes. She defines the affective response of the analyst as the:

> perception by the analyst of feelings and moods unrelated to his personal life and which may even feel alien to his normal way of reacting but which when placed in the context of the patient's material and the psychoanalytic setting illumine and render meaning to those transference phenomena that are in the process of being expressed consciously or unconsciously by the patient.

My personal monitoring of my affective response to my patients' material, and the supervision of candidates in training, have led me to believe that we must also be aware of the subtle distinctions in this affective response — that is to say, we must distinguish between our identification with the patient and empathy with her, as well as being aware of what we project on to the patient and what the patient projects on to the analyst. A very subtle and difficult manoeuvre!

The important task of supervision, as I perceive it, is to help the candidate to distinguish her own contribution to the therapeutic interaction arising from the transference on to her of the patient's own feelings. It is far easier to say, 'It's not me personally that she's talking about – it's her parents,' than to accept that it may be oneself – that the patient has accurately perceived an aspect of the analyst: for example, the analyst's personal moral attitudes to sexuality and other aspects of the patient's behaviour, which have to be acknowledged and worked through by the analyst. However much we may wish to stay in the position of neutrality advocated by Freud, I think that from our personal experience we must acknowledge that we are not neutral containers, and we have constantly to be aware of the boundary between our own feelings and attitudes and those of our patients. In other words, the analyst must beware of over-identifying with the patient and projecting her own problems into that patient.

I shall now illustrate some of the themes I have outlined with clinical examples taken both from my direct observation of patients when I was a physician and a dermatologist, and from my experience of analytic patients in my consulting room. I shall describe some of the clinical material that I have observed as a supervisor of analytic candidates in training.

As a consultant dermatologist in a women's hospital, I noticed that some patients with serious skin disorders did not respond to medical treatment alone but could often be helped if this was combined with an attempt to understand other problems in their lives. I came to realize that the hospital felt to them like a primitive maternal setting where patients could express transference feelings and elicit an appropriate response from the women doctors. This is in accordance with Freud's observation that the transference is expressed in any patient–physician relationship. The patients regressed safely to an infantile situation and managed to regain the most primitive form of maternal comfort: being soothed by another woman who would touch them and sympathize with their pain, as though she were a caring mother. Thus unconscious transference and countertransference phenomena accompanied the interaction between woman patient and woman doctor, based upon the patient's previous experience of basic trust in a significant object from her past.

However, the harsh realities of life, and particularly the realities of European life during the last war, were not environments in which a child could easily establish basic trust in her parents and the people around her. At that time I was asked to see a young refugee girl who looked like a very young child but was in fact fifteen years old, although she had reached neither puberty nor adolescence. She spoke a Slav dialect that no one, including myself, could understand, and was subject to uncontrolled explosive verbal outbursts during which she would barricade herself into her room and allow no one near her. The old aunt who had rescued her and brought her to England was bewildered by this child's paradoxical attitude to her attempts to be kind to her. When we met, and the child saw me, she immediately became calm and allowed me to give her all the painful inoculations and bodily care that a refugee child needed. She became extremely attached to me, and I would frequently find her waiting outside my house just to exchange a smile and a few words as her English improved. She never communicated her previous life to me, but what she did communicate was her need to be silent about it, so I never asked her.

She married young, and although she moved outside

34

London she always brought her child to see me, as if I were a warm and welcoming – but secret – parent; she did not share my existence with anyone else. When her last child reached the age at which she had first met me, my patient returned in deep distress. By then I had become an analyst, and she asked me for therapeutic help, since she could no longer deny her pain and her tragic past. She then told me that when the Germans had invaded her country her father had hidden her mother and herself in a village outside the town, and joined the Partisans. Mother and child were hidden by a peasant family, whose daughter became attached to the lively, rebellious child. The mother was eventually found and shot by the Nazis. The child, hidden in bed, heard the shot and saw her mother's body next day. The peasant family continued to hide her because their daughter loved her, and the Germans accepted their statement that she was their youngest child. She became silent and obedient out of fear, knowing that her previous rebellious, angry behaviour might lead to her death. We understood together that her impossible behaviour towards the aunt who had rescued her was an explosion of all that had been split off and repressed while she lived with the family that had originally rescued her. To my surprise she also brought me a photograph of her dead mother, and I recognized that physically she could have been a member of my own family. Together we understood that, triggered by a slight physical resemblance to her mother, she had immediately regained the feelings she had longed to experience. The gratification of being cared for and comforted by her mother was repeated and re-experienced in her transference to me in the present. Her attachment to me had, in its turn, stimulated the maternal, caring part of my countertransference, allowing me, in my medical care, to respond to and gratify her hidden wish.

Direct observations of aspects of the patient–physician interaction and their links with the patient's original infantile situation became much clearer to me during my training as a candidate of the British Society, and were further elaborated by my experience of the patient–analyst relationship.

I would like to illustrate this by recounting a striking episode during the analysis of one of my first patients. She had been the last child of a large family, and although she took her analysis very seriously – as I did too – something appeared to me to be missing in our relationship. She was extremely verbal and associated as much as she could, although in a rather constrained manner, and I felt that despite hard work on both our parts, she seemed to be present in person but absent at a deeper level.

After a few years of analysis, her behaviour changed in a striking way. From being an extremely verbal patient she suddenly lapsed into silence. My couch lies in the bay window of my consulting room, where the sun pours in and the patient may gaze out of the window to an aspect of trees. Since my patient was silent, I had learnt by now that I too should be silent; and at first she appeared to be very peaceful in her silence. This situation went on for about ten days, until the patient began to become restless and I too felt restless during the silence. In my mind I seemed to be preoccupied with Shakespeare's play *Macbeth* – a reminder of the text of *Macbeth* that I had studied as part of my set book for my A levels, and a play that was being studied at that time by my son. I felt rather guilty about my associations to *Macbeth*, as if my attention had wandered away from my patient, until I was struck by the recurrence of a quotation that came back into my mind most persistently with an intensity that I could no longer deny. The phrase as I remembered it was 'I was from my mother's womb untimely ripped'. As I looked at my patient, lying in tranquillity on a couch surrounded by glass, I was impelled to ask her whether she had been in an incubator after birth. She responded immediately by telling me something that she obviously could not remember, but had been told. She had been a premature baby and had spent a month in an incubator before she was allowed to go home to her mother. Through my use of the free-floating attention that an analyst brings to a session I could reach what the patient could not verbalize, and it then became clear that what was missing between mother and baby, and perhaps had never been re-established, was the early bonding in which mother and baby are as one. Thus the repetition in the transference and countertransference had repeated an aspect of the baby's and mother's non-verbalized dilemma in a verbal, yet silent, form. It seemed to me that what I had at first regarded as a pathological countertransference to my patient's silent communications was, on the contrary, a manifestation of the empathy that had been built up and now existed between us, enabling me to verbalize for her what she could not.

In contrast to this, here is a clinical vignette from the supervision of an experienced woman therapist treating a young woman patient. The therapist had an only child, a daughter, who had been separated from her during her early childhood. The mother/therapist had regained access to this daughter when she was an adolescent and an adult, and although the absence of the childhood relationship between them had left a lacuna in the therapist's life, she was delighted to have regained contact with her beautiful and talented adult daughter. The therapist, in idealizing her daughter, had also been oblivious to many of the signs of psychic pain that her behaviour was showing. It so happened that her patient came from the country in which her daughter lived, and was of exactly the same age. The patient presented herself as a beautiful and successful young woman, a view that the therapist accepted, although as her supervisor I saw no justification for the patient's view of herself, transmitted to the therapist. On the contrary, I saw considerable signs of psychic distress in her. My task as supervisor was then to disentangle the therapist's feelings towards this young woman as if she were her daughter from the patient's projection on to the analyst of her grandiose feelings about herself. What was not being reached in the treatment were the very needy parts of the patient that were protected by a defensive false-self organization. It was therefore a pathological countertransference and transference that was operating in this case. I became aware of something that the therapist herself was not aware of – her longing for her daughter to be in a close relationship with her; in order to deny the guilt of having abandoned her, she wanted to see her only as a beautiful, successful, accomplished young woman, not as a damaged one.

I would now like to remind you that there are two possible outcomes of transference and countertransference awareness. The patient may accept the transference or enter into a strong resistance against re-experiencing the painful aspects of her childhood and the relationships to the prominent figures in it. The therapist may equally encounter an unconscious strong resistance to the acceptance of countertransference which may trouble her own deepest feelings and experiences. For example, a patient may show very positive appreciation of transference feelings towards the analyst, appearing to gain insight and some change from her interpretations. The analyst may be lulled into a contented feeling that this is a good patient, and the analysis is proceeding well. My clinical experience leads me to beware of too good a patient, particularly if the patient's earliest years were spent with a depressed mother whom the patient was always trying to please and make happy.

For example, a young woman whose mother had always been depressed invariably ended her sessions with me by telling a good joke, knowing that I laugh easily. What lay behind this transference manifestation was not only an acting in the session which enabled her to leave with a visual perception of my smiling face: that is to say, she felt like a good little girl who made her depressed mother laugh, and she could then leave without guilt. It also hid an aspect of her infantile situation which she was ashamed of and wanted to deny. As this transference attitude was understood, interpreted and worked through, my patient began to show strong resistance to the transference, and to my interpretation of it. What lay behind her wish to keep the mother and me happy in the transference was a despair that her own feelings and needs would never be met. She was terrified of her secret anger and her shame at exposing the frustrated bad child hidden inside her. Gone was the good girl; in her place was an angry, snarling child who quarrelled with whatever interpretation I made and whose anger aroused enormous irritation and anger in me – countertransference feelings which I knew I must control in order to help my patient. As we worked through this phase of her analysis we understood that what was happening between us was a reverse transference, as described by King (1978) – that is to say, I was to be put in the position of a young child who could barely contain my response to a depressed mother who could come to life only when she exploded in anger, or quarrelled, or contradicted her child. My instinct was to resist the transference, yet I was constantly pulled into a position where I could either be the child who hid her anger in order to placate the mother, or explode into being the mother whom the patient had experienced as a child. Either way, the working-through and freeing from the infantile position would not have been achieved.

After some months of this situation, the patient came with a very painful personal problem. As she told me about it, she said that during the weekend she had been thinking that my response to her pain would be to behave as her mother had done, yet she knew that I would not, and in fact I did not. Our intense work on the transference–countertransference feelings – repeated in the handling, in the analytic situation, of the relationship between her mother and herself – had now achieved a change both in her and in her expectations of a response from someone else. This was reflected in her marriage, and an increasing ability to be close to her husband.

None of us is immune from the blows of human existence. Loss, mourning, physical illness, ageing, are common to analyst and patient alike. Empathy and identification are easily mobilized in the analyst's countertransference when the patient is struggling with these universal situations in her own life. However, other aspects of the patient's transference – a psychotic transference or a perverse one – may present the analyst with considerable difficulties in her countertransference feelings if she cannot achieve the imaginative leap required in order to identify with and understand her patient's feelings. Again, faced with a patient whose life experience has been traumatic, and whose pain is unbearable, an analyst may be called upon to experience an unbearable countertransference and unbearable affective states in herself, beyond her own life experience. Working with a patient faced with a terminal illness who deteriorates before the analyst's very eyes is a painful experience for the analyst yet infinitely rewarding for the patient, who can feel sustained by the analyst's support. It raises the question of how much an analyst can face her own pain in order to help the patient. Again, each analyst will respond in her own way.

My own experience in working with survivors of the Holocaust leads me to believe that eventually it is impossible to repeat the unbearable countertransference feelings. Natural defences against another's pain come into play, and the countertransference is resisted. All one can do is to accompany the patient on her journey into the past and support her in the present, in the hope that she may learn to exist again.

In conclusion, although there are many royal roads to the unconscious besides Freud's original and invaluable interest in dream life, my own analytic experience has led me to believe that the careful monitoring of the infinite variety of transference and countertransference phenomena that are revealed in the course of an analysis are amongst the most creative and exciting aspects of our work. Yet at the same time these phenomena remain some of the most intriguing, bewildering and confusing aspects of our therapeutic endeavour; they engage the analyst in constant re-examination of her own internal world as well as that of her patient. And I shall leave you with a question that a patient asked me the other day: 'Is transference love real love?' I hope you will find the answer.

ADOLESCENT PROMISCUITY:
A Clinical Presentation*

My aim in this paper is to demonstrate the predominance of aggressive impulses, wishes and fantasies in an eighteen-year-old girl, and how closely they were linked with her sexual drives.

At the time of referral, Maria had been wildly promiscuous. She sought help because of sleeping difficulties; her constant fear of dying; her inability to study when she was on her own. Latent reasons for referral were depression and a low sense of self-esteem.

Maria was a pretty, well-groomed eighteen-year-old who created an impression of sophisticated adulthood, just as she used her mature body to express superficially age-appropriate heterosexual appetites. Both her personality and her apparently normal sexuality proved to be

---

* Presented to the British Psycho-Analytical Society in a Symposium on Aggression and Sexuality, 17 March 1976.

brittle shells covering a vulnerable, frightened child, afraid of aggression in herself and in others.

She was the eldest child of a white family who had lived in Africa. Her mother breastfed her for five months, and said later that Maria had been a projectile vomiter for some of this time. Her body, from the beginning, was exposed to somatic tension after taking food, and was relieved only through violent expulsive movements. Successive nannies looked after Maria and her younger brothers and sisters, so Maria received little continuity of maternal care. She was reported to have shown intense sibling rivalry, and often smacked her siblings and nannies. When she was three she was riding pickaback on her nanny when a drunken man attacked them with a broken bottle. Her childhood was also marked by a traumatic illness at the age of six: a severe attack of bulbar poliomyelitis. When she was twelve, the family were forced to leave Africa for political reasons. She was angry with her parents for precipitating the move, and cried incessantly. She had been a bright student, but she did badly at school in England. She began to take drugs. Her first sexual encounter was at the age of sixteen.

When I saw Maria she accepted treatment readily, but from the beginning this acceptance was marked by a strong need to control both her affects and me. She sat in a chair, smoking incessantly, and talked about her problems as if she were speaking of someone else. Her parents and sisters were idealized as the happy, united family. Her mother was never criticized, and I felt that her previous sibling rivalry was turned into reactive motherliness. Only towards her seductive father could she occasionally show rage, which was often displaced in her controlling behaviour with boys. She would use her attractive body to pick them up when she felt randy, and discard them equally easily. Thus she could control the situation and leave when she chose. With older men she played a Lolita role, offering her body as though she were a pretty little girl. She excited these men in foreplay, then refused penetration, telling them to control themselves.

Maria's sexual experiences were her main outlet for aggressive feelings and wishes. They provided an opportunity to become excited and lose bodily control – although she never achieved full orgasm – and to lose verbal control after the experience by being quarrelsome and argumentative. It was only then that her self-esteem was restored and she felt completely at peace, since she had been the castrator rather than the castrated one. Loving feelings and a mature object relationship were nonexistent.

The first year of analysis was spent in establishing a treatment alliance and working through some of Maria's massive denial of aggressive feelings and wishes. Eventually she could go to sleep by using my voice as an auxiliary ego. She would say to herself, 'Sleep is not death.' At the end of the first year she reported her first dream, in which she was in a car trying to drive and control it. Her father was running alongside, trying to help her. She felt very guilty about him. In her associations she remembered her anger with her father for telling someone that she had cried on seeing him in prison. Her thoughts then went to her experiences in hospital, where she had been terrified of wetting the bed and being scolded by the nurses. She remembered her faeces and urine being drawn out of her body into glass vessels and carefully disposed of, since they carried dangerous infection, so her body felt as if it contained only dangerous and shameful matter. She recalled sitting in the back of the car when her father had run over a man and broken his leg; she had been told that the man had later died. The previous evening she had been thinking of lying on the couch, and how she resisted it: to lie on the couch was to lose control of her body and her emotions; this was dangerous and would make her feel helpless.

After this dream much of the material about her polio hospitalization emerged, including the traumatic experiences of tubes being forcibly inserted into practically every orifice, despite her struggles. She had noted that parents were allowed to visit only when their children were dying, and was therefore terrified when her father appeared dressed in a white coat, as if he were a doctor and was secretly visiting her in disguise. To her terror, on the day her father came, the little girl opposite died.

We could begin to understand Maria's pleasure and guilt at having her father to herself in this secret, exciting way, but that excitement linked with her father also brought death in its wake. Her mother did not come because she was pregnant, and some months later she gave birth to her last child. Maria had seen her absence as another abandonment, and the birth of the child made her experience further humiliations, since her mother could give birth to her father's baby, while she herself could only be sick and ill. We understood now how important it was for Maria to deny her helplessness, to regain control of her body and her feelings, and to turn passive into active.

When this dream had been interpreted and worked through, and her trust in the analyst as father was established, Maria, at the end of that first year, could begin to lie on the couch. Her aggressive feelings were increasingly verbalized instead of being turned against herself in depression or lowered self-esteem. With this, her promiscuity diminished markedly. Her body was no longer her only vehicle for expressing emotions, and she was now less anxiety-ridden and could study. She obtained a university place.

Maria verbalized a fantasy that had obviously had wide repercussions in her life. She was lying paralysed in her bed, with tubes sticking out of her. Her mother was arguing logically that she was dead, and that the tubes should be disconnected, but her father wept and begged her to let Maria live. Her guilt about her normal childhood wishes to take her mother's place as her father's sexual partner and mother his children was contained in this fantasy where her mother was punishing her by depriving her of life. The fantasy also illuminated her wish to identify with the calm logical women, her mother and her analyst, despite her fear that they were enemies. Negative feelings could never be expressed verbally in the transference, only in a bodily manner – she acted out feelings of rage at holiday separations, for example, by staying away before and after. At the same time her death fears also increased before and after the holiday breaks. The fantasy also contained her feeling that she must remain a little girl and not become a woman to challenge her mother or her analyst. Her promiscuity could then be seen as a compromise solution between her wish to be a sexually active adult woman and her fear of aggressive competition which would incur her mother's powerful revenge. We could also understand that her polio had seemed to her a punishment for smacking her sisters and being aggressive to the maids, as well as for oedipal wishes. If the tubes represented the umbilical cord, then her mother had never wanted her to live, so her pseudo-sexuality could be seen as chiefly anxiety-driven. It represented a compromise between flight from her father and refuge with a man who was like him. Most of all the fantasy represented her feeling that she could never leave her parents, since she had no separate self and could never become an individual or be alone.

Following the analysis of these defences and the freeing of her aggressive wishes and feelings, we entered the second year and phase of treatment. Maria's life changed radically. She went to university, did well academically, and found – to her joy – that she could be alone. For the first time in her life she fell in love. She could show John, her fellow student, tenderness and love, not just aggression, and this was her first mature object relationship. She was appreciative of her improvement, and her death fears and wishes disappeared. She realized that her hatred of her father had begun when she was taken to see him in prison, and they had both cried.

Unfortunately for Maria, at this point I was suddenly ill myself, had to go into hospital, and stopped work for two months. She wrote me some tense letters, and when I came back she protected me from any feelings of rage. These were split off and acted out with John, with whom she became demanding and regressed. She had also turned the aggression against herself, since her death fears had returned and this time the voice at night no longer helped. She did badly academically, but for the first time she could express aggressive, reproachful feelings towards her analyst as if she were her mother. Her aggressive fantasies now centred around her genitalia. She feared intercourse with John and began to demand reassurances from him, from her family, and from myself, as she felt she could no longer control her aggression. She sobbed, 'I killed you many times, but I never wished you sick.' She began to realize that what she wanted from John were the early satisfactions of being cuddled, stroked and held like a baby. Pseudo-adult sexuality was the only way she could achieve this pleasure, and penetration was the price she paid for it; but it was only on penetration that she became frigid and terrified, since it reawoke her terror of body intrusion, castration and disintegration. She said, 'It makes me feel as if I've lost the rational part of my mind and I'm afraid of losing control of my body and attacking and being attacked, but if I don't have a boyfriend I feel a void.' Here again we began to understand her difficulty in distinguishing whether she was victim or aggressor.

As Maria regressed, the oral origins of her sexuality became more marked. She squabbled over food with her siblings. She began to vomit before intercourse and to fear that her body was vulnerable, and could easily be damaged by John. Again her thoughts turned to her father in the white coat when she was ill, and she said, 'Now I realize it is a boy who can save me and a boy who can kill me.' Following this session she was much relieved, but after her next sexual intercourse she began to sob and cry desperately, saying, 'I don't know if I'm frigid or impotent.' What she could no longer deny was that her body contained a void, and bad and dangerous faeces and urine. Now began a time of mourning for her lost penis. She went to bed for a week, as if she had been very ill, cried a great deal, and insisted on John nursing her. When next they resumed sexual relationships, there was no weeping, but a feeling of calm and acceptance of her own femininity. She jokingly said to him before lovemaking, 'You won't kill me, will you?'

Now Maria could disclose some of her sadistic sexual fantasies to me. For example, she had a pain low down in her body for a few weeks and felt that her body was all dark, and if she let go and lost control, large jagged pieces of glass would come from inside her and damage both John and herself. The fear of the penis contained the projection of the dangers inside herself. The relationship with John began to deteriorate, since Maria realized that he was exactly like her father and treated her in the same

48

seductive way, but claimed that he needed to have his freedom to see other girls. She was aware of her hatred of him, and at times she was horrified by her barely repressed incestuous fantasies. She felt that she could no longer endure the sado-masochistic relationship or the constant fear of abandonment, and decided to leave him.

We entered the third phase of the analysis. Maria did not replace John, since she could now be alone, but having abandoned him she regressed rapidly and her fragile defences crumbled with terrifying rapidity. Gone was the cool, sophisticated outer shell, and a terrifying rage emerged. She behaved like a hungry, deprived child, sleepless, manic and persecuted. Her rage was expressed in reproaches to her mother for her lack of motherliness, and for abandoning her by going to work. She raged at me for my illness and for having abandoned her then, and strode about the room or cried aggressively and loudly. Sadistic fantasies emerged in which she was a tiny baby crawling over her father asleep in the grass in Africa. As she crawled, she cut him ferociously with a sharp piece of glass. The blood poured out, but he slept on unharmed and undisturbed. No vestige of adult sexuality remained, since the new objects of her rage were both mother and analyst. Finally, she turned the full force of her aggression against herself and lay in bed at home, begging her mother to kill her or threatening to kill herself by starvation. She broke some windows at home. In the end her suicidal wishes were so strong and her aggression towards her total self was so acute that she had to be admitted to hospital, where she remained for some months.

When she came out she went to a residential hostel and refused to see her family. We had met regularly while she had been in hospital, and now resumed more intensive treatment. Whilst she was in the hostel she always slept with a boy to protect her, but there was no sexuality, since again the wish was to hold and be held. She told me that this had begun when she had come home after her polio and a little boy had cuddled her and bathed her, for her parents had taken very little notice of her at the time. Her first seduction at sixteen had, in fact, been preceded by being bathed. In the wish to be held there was also the wish to be protected from her own strong wishes to commit suicide.

Nevertheless, there was one more suicidal gesture, and then her rage emerged in the transference: I felt literally sucked dry; my interpretations were vomited out by her, as she had vomited her early feeding and her vagina had expelled the penis. Numerous fantasies about her own body oozing pus or being full of disease preoccupied and disgusted her, so that she was unable to allow any man to come near her. At times she tried to provoke my anger almost unbearably; at other times she turned her aggression against herself in psychosomatic symptoms. Occasionally it was not enough to storm verbally at me, and she longed to hit me.

After some stormy months, which felt like a battle for control between us, Maria began to recover from the regressive process. She moved into a flat with other girls, and went back to university. She began to enjoy a sense of personal identity separate from her parents, and the fantasy of being paralysed was no longer acted out. She was more real than I had ever known her. A new pleasurable capacity for genuine care and concern for her family and her friends now encouraged her to try to understand the origins and aims of her sadism and aggressive rage that she had defended against for so long.

Maria's greatest difficulty, again, was her inability to have a relationship with a man, and this was the main focus of our work for the next few months. Because of her sexual anxieties she could no longer replace me with a sexual partner. Shoplifting was substituted for promiscuity. Frustration and rage were expressed by smashing crockery. What impressed us both was that she went home to smash crockery – she knew her calm, logical mother would be able to control her there. Maria suddenly realized that she had been able to have sexual relationships culminating in orgasm only at home, knowing that her mother was in the house and would be an auxiliary ego to control her. She now knew that it was her fear of her own blind, murderous rage that made her avoid sexuality and orgasm.

Further material about her hospitalization came into the analysis and highlighted the defensive nature of her aggression. She remembered overwhelming rage in hospital, but she couldn't scream because the nasal tube prevented her. She realized that in fantasy she had thought it was her rage to stay alive that had defeated death. Rage made her feel strong in moments of helplessness, and rage in intercourse came at that moment when she felt controlled by her partner's penis; this made her feel paralysed, unable to move, as she had felt with polio. She said, 'It is my rage that makes me feel that I'm not just a body but I'm alive inside.' Again the envy and rage with her father, who could go in and out of the hospital as he pleased, was projected on to her sexual partner, whose erection could control the whole sexual experience, no matter what she did. In addition, the envy of her father also contained the fantasy that he could control and humiliate her idealized, omnipotent mother with his penis as she herself had never been able to do, since it felt as if her mother was always abandoning her for work, for babies and for politics.

After this, Maria was contented and relatively peaceful. She enjoyed studying and found a new boyfriend. Even though he often left her for trips abroad, she no longer felt abandoned or threatened with disintegration. She decided that after she had graduated she would go to the States, so we fixed a date for termination. A new feeling of urgency entered the analysis. When she was anxiously awaiting her exam results, sadistic fantasies reappeared, but this time they were not split off and acted out with a man, but brought into the transference. For example, seeing empty milk bottles outside the door of my house, she raged that she would smash them over my head and make it crack and bleed; but as she said it she could laugh, knowing it was a fantasy, and say, 'I'll soon hold the London record for breaking bottles.' The aggression turned against herself again in moods of depression, or against me in the analytic sessions. Once her wish to scream was interpreted, scream she did in a terrifying way. For two sessions it was just as if there were two people on the couch – one with a deep, shouting, angry voice; one with a high-pitched, logical, cold voice. We were both exhausted by the tension.

The third session was calm and peaceful, as if an orgiastic relief had been obtained. We understood that what Maria had brought into the transference was the orgasm, like an anal explosion that she was near achieving with her lover but afraid to trust him with. Now a flood of memories were released – of the pleasure and stimulation by the rectal thermometer in hospital, resulting in a relief of tension in the paralysed child who could not even suck her thumb. During intercourse her anus felt as responsive and stimulated as her vagina. I suggested to her that what she was afraid of was not only losing control over aggressive thoughts and fantasies but losing control of her bowels, and infecting and damaging the whole object world. To my surprise, she answered that in fact the previous day, when she was 'stoned', she had gone to the toilet to vomit, and had uncontrollable diarrhoea all over the floor. To her surprise her depression had lifted at that moment, as if to expel all the contents of her body, and to survive, had been a moment of immense relief. She had smoked a joint after that and told me, 'It suddenly seemed to me that it was like a penis, and it was lovely. I wanted to kiss it, fondle it, and when I put it in my mouth I felt a moment of panic, thinking, "Will it hurt me?", but answered myself, "Of course not, it's wonderful; it feeds me and keeps me warm".'

The breast/penis, milk/semen equations became obvious. What I had represented in the transference was not only the fussy Jewish mother whom she longed for and never had, but also the object behind both father and mother – the African nanny. It was she who had fed Maria, cared for her body, accepted her urine and her faeces, chased her with a knife, hit her, but also cuddled her. The shouting, angry, emotional person she had always thought to be her father was also her nanny, whom she had loved and never mourned. She knew that love and sexuality could bring her to life, but she preferred emotional death, for if she were dead then hate and rage, painful as it had been, had defended her against the greater psychic pain of separation and losing the loved object, and accepting the necessity of mourning, grief and sadness.

Many of Maria's psychosomatic symptoms returned in the last months of analysis, and frightened her. She would describe the sheer physical pain of experiencing rage. She would develop crippling stomach pains or feel absolutely paralysed in her throat, strikingly repeating the physical symptoms of her vomiting and hunger as a baby, and of her poliomyelitis. Death fears returned but also, with them, her understanding of how she defended against feeling love, for to feel love was to risk disintegration and annihilation. Her pseudo-independence, aggression and

53

sophistication had been a false self that she had developed because she had been expected to mature too early in her life. Nevertheless, despite her intellectual understanding, her terrifying rage and fear of love was again acted out in every sphere where she was near success.

I said to Maria, 'How frightened you seem to be of success anywhere – in work, in love, or in your analysis.' At this she got up from the couch, shouting furiously, 'I haven't listened. I don't want any part of this competitive world. I don't want to compete with my mother or with you. I'm frightened of breaking up.' I said it seemed as if she were frightened of breaking into pieces, either with orgasm or with rage, since it felt as if all must end in disintegration and annihilation, but so much of her was more integrated than it had ever been. As I said this she sat facing me, crying desperately. She felt that her parents had never bothered to put her together after polio. She had wanted to be treated as a sick baby, but no one had recognized this or had time for her, so she had looked for it in her sexual relationships.

Following this session, the material that was worked through was her painful relationship to her mother. She felt that her mother merely produced babies, which she dropped as though they were anal babies and then went on with her own life. Maria had always felt superfluous to her mother's life. A dream at this time suggested that Maria felt that it had been her omnipotent rage which had destroyed maternal care, had made her mother give up feeding her and leave her in the care of her father and African nannies. We could also understand how important it had been for me to be able to withstand her murderous rages and attacks, and to survive; and how my illness had reinforced her anxieties about the omnipotence of her destructive wishes. After this dream, Maria went

54

home determined to talk to her mother about their relationship.

From that moment a much closer relationship between mother and daughter ensued, bringing more dreams and fantasies in its wake. Maria dreamt of two figures and a penis lying on the ground. She picked up the penis, but didn't know which figure to fix it on. She dreamt that a little white girl Maria and a little black boy Maria were running in a field in Africa when they came to a wide stream. The little white girl jumped over and ran on, but the little black boy Maria fell in the stream and was drowned. We understood from these dreams how confused Maria had been about her own sexual identity. She had used the castrating masculine aspects of herself to protect her vulnerable female identity. Now we could understand her cry of 'I don't know if I'm frigid or impotent', since in intercourse she was afraid of the excitement in which she lost control of her body boundaries and did not know if she were victim or aggressor, male or female. We also understood that it was not penetration she was so much afraid of but penile withdrawal, which left her with a vulnerable orifice. Her frigidity served the denial that her partner had a penis and she had a vagina. Instead, both remained sexually undifferentiated children. The dream also showed the split in her maternal image; she displaced all the aggression on to her nanny whom she hated and despised even though she had cared for her body, while her mother was seen as rational, and as having taught her children to think. So, in fantasy, first her father and then her male sexual partners represented the black maternal figure whom she longed for but then despised and rejected.

But there was another dimension to the dream which explained another facet of Maria's promiscuous behaviour. She told me something she had repressed throughout her analysis. She thought she had had an elder brother who had died before she was born, and who was therefore buried and left behind in Africa – hence the little black boy who was drowned in the stream – but nobody ever spoke of him, so in addition it seemed as if she had survived not only the children in hospital but also her own brother. We could now understand more about the early paralysis fantasy in which mother calmly cut the life-giving tubes, and Maria's reproaches that she was not a real mother but rather the representative of death, since she had let her own son die. We could also understand the promiscuity as the acting-out of a repressed fantasy having to do with the existence of an older brother; her guilt about it, as if her sibling rivalry had retroactively killed him; the reparative measure of bringing back a son to her parents, but also the impossibility of achieving orgasm as a permanent relationship with such an incestuous object, since to live herself she would have to kill the object.

After this material had been worked through, Maria felt that she had a right to live. She was tranquil and felt that death would come eventually, but not for many years.

Despite a very painful analysis and her previous promiscuity, I should like to stress that Maria was a most faithful and persistent patient throughout her four and a half years of treatment. I think, looking back, that despite her severe disturbance this indicates that there was a basically healthy core in her development, probably due to the fact that as her first dream shows, her father had remained a constant figure throughout her many problems and his love had given her ego strength. Nevertheless, her infantile feeding difficulties seemed to me to have laid the foundation for a somatic reaction pattern, so that her body was used to express primitive aggressive expulsory activities. As a toddler she dealt with sibling rivalry or frustration with a maternal substitute by smacking hard, so again her body was used for affective expression; but as her nanny smacked her in return, she experienced hurting and being hurt within normal limits. So she advanced rapidly to the phallic stage. The acceptance of the penile thrust implies an acceptance of being beaten rather than beating, but here she fares less well. In Maria's case, a woman being attacked and beaten, as her nanny was, not only reinforced primal-scene fantasies but gave her a traumatic bodily experience of identification with the victim – perhaps a fusion with her, since she was riding on the victim's back. At the same time, however, she was also the aggressor, since she too had hit her nanny, on to whom she had split off her frustration and her aggression in order to keep her mother as a good object. Here was her confusion as to which role she would play.

Her poliomyelitis occurred at the height of her oedipal rivalry, when her aggressive wishes were directed towards her mother, and it seemed to her as if her illness was the punishment for them. So she experienced the guilt of the oedipal triumphs, since her father came on his own to see her. Her experience of muscular paralysis was so intense – she could not control her speech, her mouth, her bladder or her anus, and most of all she could not control her father and mother – that it left a deep narcissistic scar, and made her regress. In addition, as an immobilized child she could find no outlet for the aggression which mounted within her – she could not even suck her thumb. Her sadistic fantasies were not only the outlet for her aggression but also made her feel omnipotent and destructive rather than helpless and weak. The actualization of her infantile sexual fantasy that she and her siblings were anal babies confirmed her fears that her inner world as

57

well as her body cavity was filled with only shameful, dirty, dangerous objects, and her humiliation was completed when her mother produced a healthy baby some months later. But although much of the regression in the sexual sphere and the diminution of ego strength centred around her anal phase, retroactively it also revived guilt about oral greed and envy which she felt had made her mother abandon her in the earliest months of her life, so that the greed and hunger she defended against orally were expressed sexually through her greedy vagina.

A penis wish can be exchanged for and reconciled with the possession of a vagina and its internal pleasures if what has been lost at every stage of libidinal growth is replaced with alternative satisfying and satisfactory gains, so that there is no envy for what the other has. In Maria's case this had been partly successful, since she was able to use her sexuality to some extent, although it was partly counterphobic. The major trauma was her illness and its heightened aggression, accompanied by ego weakness and dependence. Fear had made her unable to find a permanent solution or to integrate her sexuality, since to accept passivity was to accept death; so each new object revived aggression in her and made her take flight both from it and herself. It was a most painful deprivation, because Maria, like every young girl, longed for a permanent loving relationship.

Yet her earlier severe childhood illness had traumatized her so severely that her adult emotional development towards maturity was constantly disturbed by it. Her fixation to this earlier stage was worked through in her analysis, thus enabling her to resume emotional growth.

PREGNANCY AND MOTHERHOOD:
Interaction between Fantasy and Reality*

For many women the outcome of pregnancy and childbirth may be a tremendous shift towards greater maturity and an increase of self-esteem; for others, however, there may be more pathological solutions, ending in a potentially harmful and guilt-laden early mother–child relationship. The situation of the young pregnant woman and that of the earliest mother–child relationship have been vividly described by Bibring *et al.* (1961), Benedek (in Anthony and Benedek, 1970), Deutsch (1944), Caplan (1961) and other writers. In considering their views, and in relating them to my own experience of treating pregnant women and young mothers in psychoanalysis and psychotherapy, I have

---

* Based on a paper given to the Applied Section of the Institute of Psycho-Analysis on 22 March 1972, and published in the *British Journal of Medical Psychology* (1972) 45: 333–42.

come to speculate on the possibility of anticipating a pathological outcome in certain types of cases and thus, by timely intervention, avoiding the unhappiness of puerperal depression.

First pregnancy, in particular, is a time of stress for a young woman in whom the psychic equilibrium required to deal with the ever-present demands of a helpless, dependent human being has often not been permanently and securely established. One of the most impressive features to be observed during the analysis of pregnant women is the re-emergence of previously repressed fantasies into pre-consciousness and consciousness – and their fate once the reality of the newborn baby has been established. These uneasy conflicts belonging to past developmental stages are revived, as they are at any crisis point in human life, and the young woman has to achieve a new adaptive position within both her inner world and the outer object world. At this time she is in need of both emotional and physical care and support, so that she in her turn can pass on to her child the help and support in facilitating adaptation to life that she herself received. The essential adaptation in her move towards maturation is the achievement of a stable and satisfactory balance between her unconscious fantasies, daydreams and hopes, and the reality of her relationship to herself, her husband and her child.

Pregnancy, particularly the first pregnancy, is a crisis point in the search for a female identity, for it is a point of no return, whether a baby is born at the end of term or the pregnancy ends in abortion or miscarriage (Caplan, 1959; Erikson, 1959). It implies the end of the woman as an independent single unit and the beginning of the unalterable and irrevocable mother–child relationship. One of the intrapsychic tasks the young pregnant woman has to accomplish involves the internal acceptance of what may be termed the representation of her sexual partner, both physically and mentally (Deutsch, 1944). This entails a fusion of new libidinal and aggressive feelings with those already established by her childhood experiences, and in particular by her relationship to her parents and siblings, and to her own body (Bibring *et al.*, 1961; Deutsch, 1944).[1]

Fortunately, pregnancy is not a static condition but an ongoing process, both physiologically and emotionally, thus involving the emotional investment or cathexis of a developing and changing foetus, which is at first an unseen part of the mother's body and an extension of herself. This same cathexis has later to be translated into the reality of a live baby once it is born and becomes a separate part of the object world, and an extension of the sexual partner as well as of the mother herself. Thus the young mother needs not only to achieve this step, but also to prove her ability to share such an emotionally charged relationship with the father.

For the woman who is expecting her first child pregnancy offers proof of a gender identity and the visible manifestation to the outside world that she has had a sexual relationship. Physiologically it is the confirmation that she has a sexually mature body capable of reproduction, but this does not necessarily imply that she has an equally emotionally mature ego capable of undertaking the responsibilities and demands of parenthood. Hormonal changes which accompany pregnancy produce unaccustomed mood-swings and physical discomforts which impose an added burden on the pregnant woman, and possibly on those around her.

For the future mother such an enormous change, both physically and emotionally, is a normal critical transitional phase (Rapoport, 1963), and is thus inevitably accompanied by a revival of past conflicts and anxieties which add to her burden. However strongly her husband and family may identify with her at this stage, the mother's changing emotional life also imposes an alteration of relationships within a family unit, so that each pregnancy and birth must inevitably be accompanied by a normal family crisis and end with the absorption of a new family member.

Pregnancy is a major testing point of the mother–daughter relationship: the pregnant woman has to play the role of mother to her own child whilst still remaining the child of her own mother. The early childhood identifications with her own mother are reawakened and measured against the reality of her relationship to her own child. At the same time her relationship to her mother may in reality change and mature with her newfound understanding of the tasks demanded of motherhood. Thus the old ambivalent identification may be resolved, and a new and more peaceful relationship take its place.

The successful achievement of a feminine sexual and gender identity can be strengthened by the proof and confirmation of pregnancy, whereas the process of making a new form of object relationship – motherhood – can begin only once the baby separates from the mother's body, and emerges into the object world. The child thus combines an extension of the mother's self-representation and of her sexual partner, but also has to be seen as a separate individual. This complicated process and the variations to be achieved within it comprise one of the major tasks required of the young mother.

For the purposes of this paper, the nine months of normal pregnancy have been divided into three stages (Caplan, 1959).

Stage 1

From inception until the baby begins to move: approximately the first four and a half months of pregnancy.

Physiologically the progestin level is high, leading to physical malaise and changes in body ego such as the growth of the breasts, and thus reviving adolescent fantasies and feelings of body change. There are characteristically rapid mood-swings and revivals of anxiety. For some women from the very beginning of this stage there is a feeling of supreme fulfilment and pleasure, marked by an increase in libidinal investment in the self and a withdrawal from the object world, and an increase of passivity. For others, this stage may be a time of mild depression and increase of physical activity in an attempt to deny the newly felt passivity, or in accord with special problems imposed by their femininity.

For some women with more masculine stirrings there may be difficulty in accepting the increased dependence on their husbands that pregnancy and child-rearing impose. They may also feel envy of their husband's ability freely to pursue their intellectual or work ambitions if they themselves feel frustrated in continuing their own interests or chosen careers. Others may have difficulty in accepting their changing body as pregnancy progresses. In my experience, women who have felt shame and distaste over adolescent 'puppy-fat' have particular difficulty in adapting to the increase of obesity that pregnancy entails.

For some women, from the moment that pregnancy is confirmed, the foetus is cathected as a baby with an appearance and even a sexual identity, whereas for others it is a part of their body which can be dispensed with as easily as an inflamed appendix. In my opinion, this is a factor that might be of some diagnostic value in making a decision about termination of pregnancy, or in assessing the possibility of pathological mourning and depression after a therapeutically advisable abortion.

Towards the end of this first stage there is often a marked regression to the oral phase, including nausea and vomiting, and special food cravings. Often women find it difficult to feed their families at this point, thus giving the husband or other members of the family an opportunity to support and relieve the wife. The woman may also identify with the foetus as envisaged in fantasy. A young woman, joyfully anticipating the birth of her first baby, brought into her material a series of dreams in which she dreamt of herself as becoming younger as the pregnancy progressed. Finally, shortly before term, she dreamt of herself as a baby sucking at the breast, thus combining the representation of herself as the mother and as the newborn child.[2]

Stage 2

The second stage of pregnancy marks for the first time the need to face reality as the baby begins to move, thus imposing the recognition that the child, although still enclosed within the shelter of the mother's body, has to be recognized as a separate entity with a life of its own that the mother cannot control. For many women there is a moment of ineffable timeless withdrawal into their inner world when the baby moves; yet even in the most happily anticipated pregnancy there is an accompanying awakening of anxiety with the realization that eventually the baby will be a part of the external world, thus mobilizing both separation and castration anxieties in the mother. The most remarkable feature observed at this stage is the emergence of vivid regressive fantasies which would be most disturbing in other patients, yet are so predominant and commonplace in the analytic material of pregnant women. It is as if the reality of the kicking baby gives an added security to the ego, so that previously repressed primitive fantasies are allowed to emerge into consciousness very easily. Childhood sexual theories combine with conscious and unconscious fantasies, such as those in which the foetus is represented as a devouring destructive creature within the maternal body. Later, anal childhood sexual theories are revived in the notion that the foetus is something dirty or shameful that the mother needs to expel. Some women are worried by any minor change in physical well-being. A highly educated professional woman, whilst well aware that she carried a baby within her abdomen, brought previously repressed memories and fantasies relating to her shame, disgust and anxiety at having suffered from worms in childhood. A psychotic patient maintained that her enlarging abdomen was full of constipated faecal matter and wind and, when confronted by her baby at delivery, insisted that it was a large constipated stool. Such primitive fantasies may also be observed in non-psychotic patients.[3]

Towards term it is normal for the mother to envisage the foetus in the form of a baby and, as term approaches even nearer, she may envisage it as an ideal infant or growing child, often as the image of the perfect child she herself would wish to have been (Deutsch, 1944).

It is at this stage that the 'secret society of women' with its rituals and old wives' tales can be observed, and men are sometimes regarded as intruders capable of harming the child. Many women refrain from intercourse at this stage, although they remain libidinally active, as if the old fantasies of sexuality having been damaging to their bodies were revived, implying that sexual activity is potentially as harmful to the baby as it was to the mother.

A pregnant woman, whose fantasies about intercourse were of an aggressive sadistic nature, allowed her husband to have anal intercourse, although this was not her usual custom, because she feared that the thrusting movements of his penis in her vagina might damage the baby's brain. Some women fear not only intercourse but also vaginal examination by the obstetrician, as if the baby could be damaged by the hand, as they unconsciously feared damage to their own bodies due to the guilt feelings aroused by masturbation. In the analytic situation the pregnancy material may be suppressed and denied, as if exposing the baby to the analyst may also imply danger.

Fantasies of the foetus being a potentially damaging, devouring creature may occur even in the most rational of patients, and phobic anxieties may appear; for example, that the eating of strawberries might produce naevi in the baby. Certain foods are believed to be of value to the baby and certain foods harmful without any rational proof, or even in spite of medical evidence to the contrary. Rationality is of no avail, and even the most intellectual of women here re-enter the 'magic' world of childhood. A highly educated but plain woman visited art galleries regularly throughout her pregnancy to gaze at beautiful paintings in order to produce a beautiful child. Her conscious fantasy was that in this way, and in allowing herself only beautiful thoughts, she would have a perfect child.

The ego under the impact of old fantasies and unresolved conflicts of the past needs additional support from the environment, especially in primigravida, where pregnancy is experienced as a new and unaccustomed role. Here the role of the woman's real mother appears to be highly important and her support invaluable. If the real mother is not available, the husband may be used in a supportive maternal role, in addition to his role as a protective father. Other figures inside or outside the family circle may provide invaluable support. Whatever the situation of external support may be, there is neverthe-less a psychic reality, based on the early mother–child relationship that has been experienced by the future mother, which may be conflictual and in its turn deter-mines the future of the mothering in these cases. Thus motherhood is a three-generation experience. Neverthe-less, intraphysically the problem is posed as to whether the pregnant woman is to identify herself with her intro-jected mother or to rival her and succeed in being a better mother than she was felt to have been.

Stage 3

The third and final stage of pregnancy is marked by bodily discomfort and fatigue as the woman prepares for her labour. As her own need for mothering increases, in my experience memories of sibling rivalry from her own childhood appear. In the case of only children the rivalry may be displaced on to in-laws or close friends. A young woman who was pregnant at the same time as her sister-in-law had recurrent dreams in which her baby was a large beautiful boy, whilst her sister-in-law had an ugly girl.

There are characteristic mood-swings from pleasure at the imminent prospect of her baby becoming a reality to the invariable conscious and unconscious anxiety of every pregnant woman that she might die in labour, or that her child may be abnormal or be damaged during the birth. However strongly the outside world reassures her, the anxieties persist, as if old guilt feelings come into play suggesting that nothing good can be produced by her. Yet at the same time there is the beginning of an impatience and a drive to accomplish the task and bear the baby. Fantasies of expulsion from the body are more prominent at this stage, and for some women there is a feeling of exhilaration at being able again to play an active role in the delivery and to relinquish their enforced passive role during pregnancy. The most rational women may lose complete control during labour and enjoy the cathartic freedom of all the aggressive feelings, impulses and expressions available to them, as if in an orgastic experience. Yet the guilt feelings manifest themselves again in the very first question that is invariably asked by every mother after delivery: 'Is my baby normal?'

The reality of the baby emerges into the mother's consciousness and into that of the external world only when the head is being born. In my experience mothers could be encouraged to bear down by the response of the outside world, such as midwives and doctors, to the reality of the child. The curiosity aroused about the baby's physical appearance can overcome the anxiety which might otherwise cause uterine inertia.

After the birth

After delivery there is a period of adjustment to a feeling of void and emptiness where the baby once was. The mother's body image has to change once again, in order to feel whole and not empty, before there can be a reconciliation with the actual birth and the recognition of the baby as a separate individual, and yet at the same time there has to merge into this child the baby that was at one time such an intimate part of her own body. The mother may feel bewildered by not immediately feeling that the baby she sees does not evoke overwhelming maternal love. Thus the exhilaration and relief of the delivery are often followed by a period of anticlimax and depression, as may be experienced after any long-anticipated achievement. However, with the help of a supportive and sympathetic husband and family, these difficulties can be overcome. The pregnancy fantasies, and even the difficulties of the labour, are rapidly repressed and forgotten, and hopefully the mother–child relationship can be richly rewarding and satisfying to both.

I would now like to turn to deviations from normality as observed in some patients, where the early mother–child relationship shows pathological features partly due to the fantasies continuing to be acted out rather than being repressed, and to past conflicts being unresolved, thus influencing the present. Such conflicts may involve both positive and negative representations of the self and the male partner, and a continuation of ambivalent relationships to the parents and siblings of early childhood.

In the adolescent the developing awareness of the body stimulates the overwhelming impulse to use it in order to prove something to oneself, such as a sense of self-esteem through being physically attractive, or even a sense of existing because another human being acknowledges the adolescent's body as a source of pleasure. An important factor in this is the defensive splitting and bypassing of the mental processes through the use of the body – that is to say, the substitution of mental states by bodily sensations, whether for pleasure or aggressive purposes, or even as a means of avoiding depression or guilt. There is thus in these patients a splitting of different aspects of the self-representation, resembling symptoms of depersonalization which can be observed in some patients. A young patient commented: 'My body was wildly promiscuous, but inside I was a virgin white as snow.' In a study of young girls where promiscuous sexuality was compulsive (Mehra and Pines, 1972), the wish for a baby played very little part in the material, although one patient who did not become pregnant after five years of not using contraceptives became anxious about her fertility. Her anxiety was relieved and her self-esteem re-established when she became pregnant, but she immediately arranged for an abortion. In these girls the body is used in the search for an object which is never found in actual experience and contains an underlying fantasy of being looked after, cuddled and fed. Genital sexuality is the price they pay for it, and it seems fairly obvious that these girls do not enjoy being penetrated but have a tremendous pleasure in foreplay, where pre-genital infantile experiences can be revived. They are themselves in fantasy the baby, and this may be one reason why they do not wish to become pregnant. If they do they may find it extremely difficult to give a child the loving care that they themselves feel they have insufficiently received. In these girls strongly aggressive sadistic features can be observed, directed against their sexual partners, and if they become mothers, these play a part in their adaptation to the reality of a baby and can be displaced on to the child, particularly if it is a male child.

The first group of cases are of girls who embarked unusually early on sexual activity and became pregnant, thus having the inadequate resources of an adolescent, fluctuating ego with which to face the demands of the reality of motherhood. In normal adolescence there is an upsurge of regressive tendencies with a revival of old conflicts. Thus, if there is in addition an interaction with the normal pregnancy fantasies at this stage, the resultant pathology may be more severe.

Case 1

Terry, a very pretty girl, was the adopted child of an elderly couple. The only facts that she had been told about her own mother were that she had been promiscuous and that Terry had been born when she was seventeen. Terry herself was a rebellious little girl, needing to test her adoptive parents' affection, and at the age of sixteen she left home and became promiscuous. By the time she was seventeen she was pregnant and calmly set about being admitted to a home for unmarried mothers where her baby could be born and then given away for adoption. Throughout her pregnancy she was cheerful and happy, having achieved her main objects: to establish her sexual identity, to identify with her mother and turn the passive into active by having her own child adopted. The reality of the pregnancy was denied as if in a dream, and she made arrangements for the child to be adopted a few weeks after the birth. No one was available in the environment to prepare her for motherhood. The picture changed dramatically when the baby was born. Terry was stunned by the reality of a beautiful little girl with whom she strongly identified, and was deeply traumatized by having to go through with the adoption, as she had no possible means of supporting herself or the child, and had made no plans for such a future. For years she mourned her child, worried about her well-being, and was very depressed at the anniversary of her birth and at Christmas time.

Case 2

Jenny, aged twenty-three, was a student suffering from a severe character neurosis with hysterical and phobic symptoms. She was dependent and demanding towards her husband, who nevertheless loved her and tried to satisfy her needs, including her outbreaks of hysterical rage towards him as a defence against her overwhelming anxiety whenever she was left alone. Her relationship with her own mother had been difficult from her earliest childhood, and she had entirely rejected her when she left home at seventeen. During the course of therapy her phobic symptoms were strongly alleviated, her performance at her training college greatly improved and her husband was able to make rapid strides in his own profession as her demands on him became modified. Eventually they decided to have a child, and both partners were overjoyed when Jenny became pregnant. Her pregnancy was uneventful and her husband, who was present at her delivery, helped her considerably throughout. They were both delighted with their baby daughter and the whole process increased Jenny's maturational progress towards accepting her feminine role. She became a devoted and competent mother and wife, and eventually reconciled herself with her parents.

Unhappily for Jenny, she had, however, discovered that to be pregnant also carried the additional benefit for her that she need never be alone. She wished to be pregnant without the responsibility of mothering more children. Against all medical advice, she became pregnant again within a few months of her first child's birth, and it was soon discovered that this time twins were to be born. In spite of her great bodily discomfort, she was cheerful and happy throughout her pregnancy and maintained her good relationship with her child, her husband and even her mother. However, when the reality demands of feeding twin babies and an older child under two imposed themselves, she began to be depressed. Her husband could no longer help her, as he had to work longer hours in order to earn more money. She became terrified of the twin babies, who were small and hungry, and eventually she was unable to feed them at all owing to the revival of her oral-sadistic fantasies. The demanding greedy twins became the representation of the oral-sadistic aspects of herself. Under the stress of her guilt and anxiety she

72

eventually had a psychotic breakdown for which she was hospitalized and from which she never recovered, eventually committing suicide. Thus in Jenny there had been a maturational stride towards ego strength during her first experience of motherhood, but she had been unable to maintain it in the face of the added stress of additional child-rearing.

Case 3

Ruth, an intelligent graduate of twenty-five, came into analysis after a year of marriage to a supportive, maternal husband. She sought help for her anxiety hysteria, which manifested itself mainly in her certainty that she would contract cancer of the uterus and die. This had made her terrified of intercourse, because she was convinced that the sperms emitted during ejaculation were the carriers of carcinogenic material. She had elaborated many 'magic' rituals in order to avoid the danger, including regular visits to a male gynaecologist where she would resist vaginal examination and thus produce orgastic pain and spasm when an instrument was introduced. Ruth's mother had suffered from asthma, often being ill in the night, thus provoking the child's fantasies that she had been damaged by sexual intercourse whilst in bed. Ruth's father, who had been an aggressive, impatient man, committed suicide shortly before his wife's death, and both parents were dead when Ruth married. During the course of her analysis her anxieties and guilt feelings about her parents were worked through, including her oral fantasy that she had devoured and damaged her mother *in utero*. She was no longer frigid with her husband, and eventually became pregnant.

During her pregnancy the old unconscious fantasies were revived, centring mainly on her anxiety that she would be devoured and damaged by her own child as she had in fantasy damaged her own mother. Throughout the first three months her feelings of triumph and contentment at having proved that, like her dead mother, she could become pregnant and have a child maintained a peaceful equilibrium within her. However, when in the second stage the baby began to move, the previously analysed destructive fantasies re-emerged side by side with her strong sense of reality that the foetus was also a baby and an extension of her real self, as well as of her fantasied identification with a devouring foetus. They were not as overwhelming as they had been in the beginning of her analysis, when she had not even dared to contemplate pregnancy and childbirth. She was exhilarated in the third stage not only by the renewed activity implied in the expelling of the baby, but also by the aggressive wish to be rid of this damaging representation of her sadistic wishes towards her mother. These were successfully worked through, and with the birth of the child the fantasies were repressed – Ruth became a devoted, happy mother, and enjoyed and appreciated her husband. Without analytical help she would never have been able to contemplate pregnancy and would probably have become severely depressed and committed suicide, as her own father did.

Case 4

Eva sought help on the advice of her mother, who had been treated by me in supportive therapy many years earlier when she became pregnant by accident in middle age. She had at first decided to have an abortion but later changed her mind, and with therapeutic help went through with her pregnancy and gave birth to a son of whom Eva was very jealous, although by then she was ten years old and could disguise it under a cloak of maternal solicitude. The mother had some problems in dealing with a male child but succeeded in working them through, and derived great pleasure from her son.

At the time of her referral, Eva was pregnant for the third time. She had married at the age of nineteen and, although frigid at first, had succeeded, with the help of her understanding husband, in establishing a happy marriage. Her first child, a girl, was a source of great pleasure to her, being the representation of the pretty girl that she herself had been and indeed still was. She was therefore loved and appreciated as an extension of herself. The second child, a boy, was born with a mild infantile eczema which repelled her. Furthermore, he was a crying, demanding baby, later growing into an unhappy, clinging toddler. To her distress Eva compulsively rejected this child, punishing him for any misdemeanour, and was unable to give him any physical affection in spite of her great effforts to control her behaviour. When she became pregnant for the third time, Eva worried that if the third child were to be a boy she might again be impelled to reject him and, encouraged by her mother, came to consult me. It was interesting to see the mother's difficulties repeated by the daughter again in relation to a male child, and indeed, as Eva's pregnancy progressed and the inevitable absorption in her pregnancy entailed less attention to the object world, the little boy's demands increased and she was disturbed by her mounting resentment and irritation at him, whereas she was patient with her daughter.

During the course of analysis the sibling rivalry with her younger brother was worked through and her relationship with her child improved. As she showed him open affection he became less demanding and dependent, and made strides towards independence which greatly pleased his mother and grandmother. It then became apparent that the boy not only represented her rival in early childhood, but that his eczema had revived previous fantasies about her own body. Her mother had been severely ill with ulcerative colitis during Eva's early childhood, and this had influenced Eva's fantasies of childbirth – that she and her brother had been anal, dirty, offensive products of a sick mother. Her own son's eczema, which she equated with dirt, had produced in her not only the revulsion she had felt about her sick mother's body but also her anxiety that her mother's disease would be repeated in herself and shown in her own or her children's appearance.

It was Eva's strong maternal concern for her child which made her feel that her rejection of him was in keeping neither with her picture of herself as a woman, nor with her memory of her own mother. She did not want to harm him or the next baby, as she knew she might do if her compulsive aggression were allowed to continue. Her trust in her own mother enabled her to seek help where she had once been helped herself.

Conclusion

The task a woman has to accomplish in pregnancy and motherhood is to integrate reality with unconscious fantasy, hopes and daydreams. She has, in addition, for the first time to meet the demands of a helpless dependent creature who represents strongly cathected areas of self and non-self, and many past conflictual relationships. This task may prove overwhelming, especially in the case of a very young, inexperienced woman. Support at this time from the environment is invaluable, especially from the husband, mother or any valued interested person. As crisis intervention can bring such valuable help, particularly in the absence of adequate family support, it would perhaps be useful to bear these factors in mind not only in the antenatal and postnatal period, but also when assessing the effect of therapeutic abortion in order to anticipate and reduce puerperal depression. Such intervention might also avoid the perpetuation of a guilt-laden mother–child relationship which could emotionally deprive the baby of a secure and satisfying foundation in life. It should, however, be emphasized that some of the cases discussed make it clear that however adequate the support from the environment may have been, the severity of the unresolved conflicts necessitated psychoanalytic or psychotherapeutic intervention in order to achieve a successful outcome.

Notes

1. It should, however, be noted that other equally important tasks involved in the preparation for childbirth and child-rearing, such as the changing interpersonal relationships, are not discussed in this paper.
2. Communication from Dr Malcolm Pines.
3. Case material from a patient treated by Dr Lionel Kreeger.

ADOLESCENT PREGNANCY
AND MOTHERHOOD*

It is striking that despite advances in contraception and the easy availability of termination of pregnancy, a considerable number of teenage girls still become pregnant, and some become teenage mothers. For many of them the normal developmental crises of puberty and adolescence, followed by that of first pregnancy and motherhood, facilitated further psychic growth. For others these crises may revive primitive anxieties and conflicts belonging to previous developmental phases, which cause them to regress. For some of these young mothers the birth of a real baby may prove disastrous. The physical maturity of puberty offers them an alternative means of resolving psychic conflict and establishing their femininity. While a girl's wish to be pregnant may be seen as part of normal adolescent development, a further step in

* Published in *Psychoanalytic Inquiry* (1988) 8: 234–51.

maturation evokes a wish to bring a live child into the world and achieve fulfilment of the maternal ego-ideal. The adolescent girls I am discussing, however, appear to have taken only the first part of this developmental step. In this paper I focus on the unconscious conflicts of some immature young women that prevent them from establishing good-enough mothering (Winnicott, 1965).

Maturational Development and Relationship to the Mother

Erikson (1959) described the maturational stages of the life cycle. Of these the uniquely feminine body changes of puberty, leading to the psychological impact of adolescence, first pregnancy, and the birth of a child, are major landmarks in a young woman's growth towards establishing a mature female identity. Each maturational step initiated by body change is inevitably accompanied by a normal emotional crisis, in so far as libidinal, aggressive, and narcissistic components of the relationship to the self and to the object must be altered in both the inner and outer worlds. Each crisis may either facilitate psychic growth or highlight fixation to an earlier phase of development. In my view the young woman's experience of her own mother – of her capacity to mother – and the way her mother has dealt with her own femininity and that of her child is of primary importance. As we have seen elsewhere, the development of a woman's mature female identity, based on the pre-oedipal development of sound self and object representations and a well-founded sense of gender and sexual identity, involves not only identification with the internal representation of her mother but also the opposite lifelong task: that of separation and individuation from her.

79

Adolescence

Laufer and Laufer (1984) view the main developmental function of adolescence as the establishment of the final sexual organization. The body's representation must now include the physically mature genitals. They see the various developmental tasks of adolescence – the change in relation to the oedipal object, to one's contemporaries, and to one's own body – as being subsumed under the principal developmental function rather than as separate tasks. A girl may undergo a turbulent time during her adolescence if her pre-oedipal experience with her mother has not led to a firmly established sense of gender identity and of self. The upsurge of emotional regressive tendencies and re-emergence of unresolved conflicts belonging to the past may impede the thrust towards her further emotional maturation and psychic growth. In adolescence feelings of self-esteem are particularly related to physical appearance and to the image of the self mirrored in positive or negative response from peer figures. However, though a young woman's newly mature and sexually responsive body takes her into the world of adult sexuality, it may also enable her to use her body to protect herself against unresolved emotional conflicts from a much earlier infantile stage of life. As we shall see in the next chapter, 'The Relevance of Early Psychic Development to Pregnancy and Abortion', sex may become a way of gaining comfort and holding that stems more from a longing for pre-oedipal mothering than from a desire for an adult sexual relationship.

In such girls, strongly aggressive and sadistic feelings towards the mother may be observed – factors that complicate the normal adolescent process of emotional separation from her. Thus ambivalence towards her may be resolved in a negative way rather than in the positive one of love. Previous childhood conflicts about identification with her are revived and reinforced (Pines, 1982), complicating the further stage of first pregnancy, in which identification with the maternal ego-ideal (Blum, 1976) is physically and emotionally attainable for the first time.

First Pregnancy

A woman's first pregnancy is an experience of deep biological identification with her mother that may reactivate intense ambivalent feelings. For a young woman whose experience with her own mother has been 'good enough', the temporary regression to a primary identification with a generous life-giving mother, as well as with herself as if she were her own child, is a pleasurable developmental phase in which further maturational integration, enhancement of self-esteem, and growth of the self may be achieved.

But for others, in whom ambivalent feelings about the mother have been unresolved and negative feelings about the self, the sexual partner, or important figures from the past predominate, the inevitable regression of pregnancy facilitates the re-emergence of previously unresolved conflicts, which had been defended against. The pregnant woman may frequently project ambivalent or negative aspects of herself and her internal objects on to the foetus as if it were an extension of them all. It follows that the special emotional state of pregnancy in which the young woman may identify with her own mother, and therefore with the wish to become a mother to an infant, is in conflict with her identification with the foetus, which naturally intensifies the universal infantile wish to be mothered again. The re-emergence of previously repressed fantasies into the pregnant woman's conscious mental life, which I have described more fully elsewhere

81

(Pines, 1972), must be taken into account, since they must be integrated with the reality of the baby once it is born. For the new object relationship, which can develop only with the newborn infant, will depend not only on the child itself, its sex, its appearance and its behaviour, which affect the mother's view of herself and of her skill at mothering, but also on the mother's concrete experiences of pregnancy and of giving birth, important stages towards recognizing in that baby outside her the foetus that was once an intimate part of her own body.

Adaptation to that baby requires the achievement of a stable and satisfactory balance between the mother's past experience of being mothered, her unconscious fantasies, daydreams and hopes for her child, and the reality of her relationship to herself, her sexual partner, and her baby. The outcome following the temporary regressive state of pregnancy may be a healthy solution and a further step towards maturation, but if the mother's psychic equilibrium has not been reorganized and the crisis is not resolved before she is confronted with the reality of her newborn child, a pathological solution may lead to a harmful and guilt-laden early mother–child relationship.

In the case of an adolescent girl whose ambivalence to her own mother has complicated both emotional identification with her and appropriate separation and individuation from her, the premature use of her physiologically mature body and its sexuality may lead to her forming immature object relationships in an attempt to resolve this problem. If this crisis is further complicated by the demands of pregnancy and motherhood it may lead to pathological solutions, difficulties in mothering and motherliness, rather than to healthy developmental growth.

Use of the Body as an Alternative Means of Separation–Individuation and Maturational Psychic Growth

A little girl's wish to identify with her mother can be seen in games and fantasies long before there is any physical possibility of having a child (Deutsch, 1945; Benedek, 1959). A sense of gender is established in early childhood; sexual identify is largely resolved by the end of adolescence. As the adolescent matures, she is taken into an important new stage of separation–individuation. The revival of intense sexual feelings drives the young girl towards her first intercourse, which confirms her right to take responsibility for her sexuality and ownership of her adult body as distinct from her mother's. In each transitional phase of the life cycle, body changes – changes in narcissism, object relations, culturally determined role patterns, and expressions of sexuality – must influence and modify the view of the self.

Winnicott (1965) emphasized the important role of the maturational environment provided by the mother in the primitive stages of ego development. The way in which she has both physically and emotionally handled the infant's body and emerging self is integrated with that child's experience and her conscious and unconscious fantasies. The representation of an internal mother created in this way is a lifelong model for her daughter to identify with and also to differentiate herself from. It is only at this early stage that the little girl can introject a feeling of mutual body satisfaction between her mother and herself (E. Balint, 1973). If the little girl has not felt satisfied by her mother at this pre-oedipal stage or felt that she herself has satisfied her mother, she can never make up for this basic loss of a primary stable sense of well-being in her body and with her body image unless she sacrifices her normal drive towards a positive oedipal outcome (Pines, 1980). Furthermore, she may remain with an unsatisfying and unsatisfactory self-image, which remains unaltered in the true self no matter how much adult experience does not bear it out. Her move towards a differentiated sexual identity, the same as her mother's and yet separate, also necessitates an internalization and identification with her mother's female body. Separate from the mother, the little girl's attempts to identify with her can be seen in oedipal wishes to bear her father's child.

Biological puberty necessitates a change of body image for the little girl from that of a child to that of an adult woman with breasts and genitalia. She must now accept her vagina as an orifice capable of holding a man's penis – in fantasy that of her mother's sexual partner, her father – and becoming pregnant.

It is my impression that adolescent girls who have experienced a lack of good-enough mothering may use their bodies in an attempt to regain the infantile state of the baby: an illusory search for a lost narcissistic state. In addition they hope to regain their ideal self in their new baby. These girls, in my view, have had mothers who could care for their daughters' bodies but could not contain their anxieties or their affects. M. M. R. Khan (1974) states that in adult life these girls use sexual activity instead of ego capacities in object relationships – a view with which I concur, for sexuality at puberty and in adolescence is based on early experience with the mother.

Clinical Material
Case 1

Mrs X became a mother for the first time at the age of sixteen. She had sought analytic help after her younger

child had been treated at a child guidance clinic. Mrs X
was severely depressed, recognized that her marriage was
failing, and felt that she could no longer carry on. She had
been the first child and only girl in her family, with three
younger brothers whom she often – angrily – took care of.
Her mother was a tough, angry woman who did not value
either her own or her daughter's femininity. No satisfactory or satisfying relationship could exist between them,
and the little girl could not love her mother's body or her
own. Mrs X's father, a coarse and violent man, valued his
men friends more than his wife or his little daughter, so
that she could not turn to him for protection or a loving
relationship. The child had been unprepared for the onset
of menstruation and felt that the flow was excretory, dirty
and painful, an impression that was confirmed by her
mother insisting that she must use old rags to contain it
rather than buy sanitary towels. Thus her femininity, her
body image and her sexuality were from the outset
strongly linked with shame and self-hatred. We might
assume that her mother also disliked her femininity and
her own body. Mrs X had always been extremely jealous
of her younger brothers who, she felt, were more deeply
loved by her mother just because they were boys. Hatred
of her mother enabled Mrs X to detach herself from her
at this stage.

Adolescence afforded her a new way of coping with life.
At fourteen she learned to use her body and her sexuality
to raise her self-esteem and experience herself as being
lovable through genital heterosexual relationships in
which she always played the seductive, active role. Mrs
X's physically mature body and her entry into adolescence now enabled her to substitute sexual excitement for
psychic emptiness and pain. She appeared to be moving
adequately towards adulthood by fulfilling the normal
developmental tasks of adolescence. She took on responsi-

bility for her mature body and her adult sexuality, and experimented with new relationships to boys in her own peer group. Unconsciously she searched for an object that would love her and raise her self-esteem, since she could not love herself or anyone else. She did poorly at school and turned even more to promiscuity as a means of bypassing her difficulty in thought or learning.

When Mrs X became pregnant at sixteen, her mother angrily arranged an abortion. Her seventeen-year-old boyfriend insisted on marrying her, but despite this her mother was still rejecting and angry. Following the wedding Mrs X and her husband moved away. After a difficult and anxiety-laden pregnancy her first child, a girl, was born. Again her young husband was supportive and helpful, thus replacing her rejecting mother, and their mutual sexual pleasure corrected her dissatisfaction with her body image and her femininity. Since he mothered her, she could in turn mother her little girl – not only as her child but as if she also were the ideal baby-self that had never been mothered by her own mother. The second child, a boy, was born in quick succession, but Mrs X's marriage deteriorated and she became frigid. Since Mrs X had always used her body to express conscious and unconscious feelings, she found it difficult to be her baby's mother and at the same time remain her husband's sexual partner. In response to his wife's frigidity, which he could neither understand nor help her with, Mr X, feeling emotionally castrated, was driven constantly to prove his potency with her. Furthermore, since he had always expressed his love towards her by his sexuality, she now responded angrily because she felt that he misunderstood her primitive needs for protection and love rather than for sexuality. The repressed problems that had preceded and accompanied her first pregnancy and the birth of her first child were repeated with this pregnancy, as they had not been worked through. Mrs X's delight in her little girl's body as if it were her own, and the mutually satisfying situation between them, had mitigated her basic view of herself and her own mother as an unsatisfactory couple. Since she angrily devalued her husband for failing to understand her need for support, the relationship with him could no longer maintain her precarious sense of adult identity as a lovable woman. She regressed to her basic view of herself as unsatisfying to an unsatisfactory object. In this way her marriage repeated her pre-oedipal situation. This last child, who now was the living proof of her guilty sexuality, was invested with the negative aspects of herself, the shameful greedy child that she felt herself to have been and continued to be in her marriage. The sibling rivalry towards her brothers and the devalued aspects of her husband were displaced on to the boy, and he became an object of dislike and aggression. It seemed that she could not see this child as an individual in his own right, nor could he become her ideal self as her daughter had, since he was the boy she could never be. We understood in the course of our work together that since thought, symbolization and fantasy were unavailable to Mrs X, in becoming a mother she became the bad mother of her experiences as well as remaining the emotional child that part of her was. Her marriage now repeated her pre-oedipal situation, as if her husband were the mother who had cared for her body but not for her feelings.

It became clear in the course of her analysis that Mrs X could not accept anything that she experienced as good and pleasurable. She used her constant criticisms of her husband and her son as a means of increasing her own very low self-esteem. By projecting on to them both everything she could not tolerate in herself, she could allow herself to go on living with them. In the transference the analyst was seen as a critical and punishing figure, and any dependence or any gain in insight led to constant threats that she would leave the analysis as if that, too, as well as attachment to the analyst, was too good and pleasurable for her. Shame was a predominant feature both in her life and in the transference. It could now be seen that her aggressive attempts to shame her husband and her son were attempts to turn passive into active, to raise her self-esteem and thereby avoid depression.

Mrs X's view of herself began to change in the course of her analysis. Her envy of her analyst and sharp observation enabled her to learn how to respect her own body more. Her appearance and her clothes reflected this improved view, as did her attempts to make amends to her husband and her son for her previous hostile behaviour. As her self-esteem improved she was able to bring into the analysis both her intense masturbatory activity, which had never ceased since early childhood, and the acting-out of a masturbatory fantasy which had always gratified and excited her. In the fantasy she was an exploited drudge in her childhood, in her marriage, and in the analysis. The theme of deprivation was further acted out in her stealing food from shops on her way to her analytic session. She became very excited over the danger of being nearly caught and still outwitting the shop assistants. It emerged that in her childhood she had stolen milk from the kitchen cupboard while her mother was breastfeeding the male siblings who were born after her. In the transference she felt that any interpretation that helped her was stolen both from the analyst/mother and from the other patients, who became her siblings. Analysis of the envy both of her mother at that early time and of her analyst's capacity to give her something valuable in the transference enabled some of these problems to be worked through.

As Mrs X's capacity to think became more available to her, she returned to work and did well in her job. She could now allow herself to experience the analyst as a caring figure who would not abandon or reject her for her misdeeds as she felt her mother had first rejected her in her childhood in favour of her siblings, and as she had again rejected her during her first pregnancy when Mrs X longed to be cared for as if she had regressed to being the baby once again. The care she received in her analysis enabled her to be more caring for her child. She could also express her pleasure in her newly permitted wish to enjoy her femininity and her feminine role, and a subtle change took place in the family constellation. Her husband responded by taking more responsibility for the family, and she could allow herself to enjoy being cared for, and no longer feel a drudge. She could also allow her mother to join in some of the newly found family pleasures, and – to her astonishment and mine – discovered that her mother, in her turn, had become pregnant with Mrs X when she was sixteen and had also had to be married for that reason.

In my experience many patients, as they come towards the termination phase of their analysis, verbalize a strong wish to conceive a child, as if, in fantasy, ending analysis is the equivalent of giving birth to a less conflictual self. Mrs X's conscious wish towards the end of her own analysis was to conceive her last child as an outcome of a new-found satisfactory and loving relationship with her husband. She learned, with rage and pain, that her daughter was now pregnant at the same age as she had been. Mrs X, after much conflict, decided to content herself with being a young grandmother.

Case 2

Mrs A had been adopted at an early age, and had a happy childhood until her adoptive mother died. The child had struggled to mother her adoptive mother through her terminal illness. She was ten when she was left alone with an inadequate, severely depressed father. On the day of her mother's death she insisted on his taking her to see her real mother who, to her astonishment, not only lived a few streets away but was rearing her brother. All her hopes of finding a replacement were shattered, since her real mother obviously wanted nothing to do with her. With both real and adoptive mothers failing her, she was left alone with hurt and angry feelings towards women. The social services placed her in a residential home, since her father was unable to keep her or his own home going. She frequently ran back to her father until eventually she was old enough to leave the residential home, and free to return to him. Puberty and adolescence afforded her a new way of coping with life. She filled the house with adopted stray animals, as if they represented the lost aspects of herself.

While she was still at school – where she could not learn, since her mind was blocked – she used her body to regain love and self-esteem. She consciously wanted to be physically cuddled and loved by a boy, which was normal adolescent behaviour, but in addition she unconsciously wanted to recover all the primitive childhood bodily pleasures, as if in fantasy he were her mother. At the same time she needed a man to distance her from the threatening sexualized attachment to her lonely father. She told me later in her analysis that she used her attractive adolescent body to provoke her father into showing her his penis. As a father he failed her by responding, and then she would control him as if she were the stronger mother who protects father and little girl from acting-out their unconscious incestuous feelings.

Mrs A's physically mature body, and her entry into adolescence, now enabled her to substitute sexual excitement for psychic emptiness and pain. She appeared to be moving adequately towards adulthood by fulfilling the normal developmental tasks of adolescence. She took on responsibility for her mature body and her adult sexuality, experimented with new relationships to boys in her own peer group, and appeared to be detaching herself from her infantile tie to her father. Unconsciously, her body experimentation contained a hopeless search for the lost adoptive mother she could not replace, and for their earliest affectionate relationship. Each sexual partner was abandoned as cruelly as she had felt abandoned by both her mothers. Eventually she seduced a young man who made her pregnant and, to her surprise, married her. She now had a man who loved her and who, in fantasy, represented both her dead mother and her sexual partner, Mrs A's living father. It should be noted that my patient was searching for someone to love her, since she could not love herself. Pregnancy enabled her to feel that she was now a mature woman like her real mother and, in addition, to have a blissful fantasy of returning to the womb, as if she were the foetus inside her own body. Now her empty body was full, and the longing for her dead adoptive mother was less intense, since she expected the baby to love her and always be with her. When the baby began to kick and she could no longer deny the coming separation that birth would impose, she became depressed and took to her bed. She knew that she would be alone again, just as she had felt alone and abandoned when death had separated her from her adoptive mother, for birth and death, both separations, are closely linked in the internal world. Thus Mrs A's first pregnancy, a further developmental phase in a woman's life cycle, became the point at which she broke down.

For Mrs A, whose son was born when she was seventeen, becoming a mother was a calamity. She often wheeled him past her real mother's house, hoping that her mother would come out to see her grandson and help her daughter to become a mother, but the miracle never happened. Left alone with her baby, Mrs A began to beat him whenever he cried or whenever she felt helpless and panic-stricken at demands she could neither understand nor satisfy. The feelings towards the child, which had begun as ambivalent, turned into hate rather than love.

We understood in the course of our work together that it was now as if she had become the bad mother of her own past experience as well as remaining the emotional child. For that child inside her the baby represented a rival in many different ways. He represented the brother her real mother had kept, while she herself had been rejected. Moreover, since her husband was a maternal figure for her, she resented his interest in the baby and envied her own child the unconditional love that he received. Any aggression she felt towards her husband or her father was displaced on to the male child, whom she abandoned whenever she could. She abandoned him as she felt she had been abandoned twice by bad mothers, for to the child she had been, death represented abandonment. But most of all, the baby represented aspects of herself that she disliked. Mrs A had wet the bed until she was pregnant, and gave it up at that stage because she felt that a mother should be clean; in being clean she became frigid, because for her genital sexuality was also associated with dirt and soiling. The baby, therefore, was the concrete proof of her dirty sexuality, and also denied her sexual pleasure. There was a helpless child outside her, crying, soiling or wetting, behaving just like the child inside her, whom she hated. She struggled hard to look after him, but from the beginning she not only hated these features of herself in the baby but also hated him for the loneliness and isolation at home that she felt was due to his birth. The birth repeated the incontinence and isolation of her adoptive mother's illness, and the baby also represented the mother who had taught her to be clean. At times these feelings were beyond control, and she battered him. But part of her was also identified with her good adoptive mother, so that she became guilty and depressed about her compulsion to beat the baby. It was at her husband's insistence that Mrs A came for help. As a result of therapy she began to understand all the child represented for her and what she projected on to him. This made it easier for her to see the baby as a real child in his own right.

Mrs A's transference was particularly devoid of affect. She presented with a smiling, indifferent face, dressed in black leather motorbike clothes, often wearing a crash helmet. Many times I felt intensely angry as she told me, seemingly without any emotion, of the behaviour that produced injuries in her little boy. He fell down the stairs, or she pushed the door in his face, knowing that he was about to crawl through it. Once when she brought him to my waiting room, I witnessed her abusiveness. My intense countertransference feelings of anxiety for the baby's safety and rage at my patient for her impassive cruelty towards him enabled me to understand the externalization on to me of the alive, angry, rejecting, cruel mother she had experienced in her real mother, and the emotional death of the kind adoptive mother within her that might have mitigated these attacks. It was as if she had lost that part of herself. In understanding her predicament I learned to become the maternal figure who emotionally held her terrified immature baby-self and so enabled her to protect her own child from her envious and sadistic attacks. My anxiety mirrored hers. Experiencing it myself enabled me not only to be in touch with her despair and the urgency of her situation, but also to understand that no one else could contain her baby-self for her as her good mother might have done – there was no viable alternative in her psychic life to a rejecting angry mother and a traumatized child. As we worked through these problems that linked her past to her present, Mrs A's maternal ambivalence towards her child was modified. She could contain her frustration and rage, and since she was no longer helplessly crushed by guilt she was able to establish a more loving relationship with her son. Mourning her adoptive mother enabled her to use her mind again, and she went back to college to complete her education.

Conclusion

I have illustrated my theme by clinical material from two patients who were adolescent mothers. I wish to stress that superficially both young women appeared to show normal adolescent behaviour, but were more deeply disturbed than they seemed at first sight. Both broke down in pregnancy, and their early mother–child relationships were deeply affected.

The transference and countertransference problems encountered in the analysis of both these patients revealed that there was no viable alternative to a rejecting mother and a rejected child. Both patients externalized a harsh, punitive superego figure which was projected on to the analyst and which they each acted out by rejecting and punishing their children. Yet at the same time it could also be understood that the secret gratification of the psychic containment that they both experienced in the analytic situation evoked intense anxieties about being trapped for ever, which in Mrs X's case prompted her to threaten angrily and repeatedly to leave. Mrs A left when her positive feelings emerged. My countertransference was an important tool enabling me to understand these problems. At first my response was to feel angry and outraged by these mothers' cruelty to their children. I felt acute discomfort at such unusually intense anger with my patients, and at my own strong condemnation of their behaviour. I was aware of an urgent desire to restore my own psychic equilibrium by punishing them verbally. Yet careful monitoring of my reactions, and of my strenuous attempts to work through these feelings in order to maintain an analytic stance, led me to believe that what was being repeated was the patients' intense activation of my maternal feelings. I was faced with a choice of behaviour. I could repeat the harsh attitudes of the punitive, rejecting mother of my patients' internal world and sadistically attack their vulnerable infantile self. Or I could protect them from what was aroused in me by their behaviour and, in doing so, understand from my own experience how difficult it was for them to protect their children from the sadistic repetition of their own infantile situation with these harsh mothers. In this way, transference and countertransference problems reflected the difficult relationship to their own mothers in which the infantile aspects had not been resolved and successfully integrated in their adult selves.

Finally, it may be of some interest to note that both patients had had a previous experience of therapy with a male therapist. Mrs A had been silent for much of that time, and seemingly unaffected by the therapy, while Mrs X had experienced an intense eroticized transference which had frightened her and caused her to leave. It seems to me that an important factor in working through some of their problems was the fact that I was a woman. I concretely offered them both a more benevolent maternal figure to introject and identify with. In addition, it seems to me that I could also, as a woman analyst/ mother, offer them permission to enjoy their female bodies and their sexuality – permission that their hostile mothers did not ever appear to have given them.

THE RELEVANCE OF EARLY PSYCHIC DEVELOPMENT TO PREGNANCY AND ABORTION*

Introduction

Freud, a man of his time, believed that pregnancy and birth gratified every woman's basic wish. The gift of a child would partially compensate for the unfulfillable wish for a penis. My analytic experience does not confirm this view. It has led me to believe that there is a marked distinction between the wish to become pregnant and the wish to bring a live child into the world and become a mother. For primitive anxieties and conflicts arising from a woman's lifelong task of separa-

---

* Presented at the 32nd International Psychoanalytical Congress, Helsinki, July 1981, and published in *International Journal of Psycho-Analysis* (1982) 63: 311–18.

tion–individuation from her own mother may be unexpectedly revealed by the emotional experience of first pregnancy and motherhood.

In this paper I shall focus on difficulties concerning a woman's identification with the internal representation of her own mother, an identification that is bodily reinforced when she becomes pregnant. I shall also discuss the revival in pregnancy of infantile fantasies about herself as the intrauterine foetus in her mother's body which are activated by her narcissistic identification with the foetus now concretely inside her own body. The physically symbiotic state of pregnancy is paralleled by an emotional symbiotic state in the future mother where identifications with her own mother, and with herself as the foetus, may reactivate intense ambivalent feelings. Pregnancy therefore affords the future mother an opportunity to decide whether to let the foetus live or die. The analysis of a patient who repeatedly allowed herself to become pregnant but aborted the pregnancy each time will illustrate this theme. Transference–countertransference problems encountered in her analysis with a woman analyst reflected the difficult relationship to her own mother in which the infantile aspects had not been successfully resolved and integrated in her adult self.

First Pregnancy

Bibring *et al.* (1961) write: 'The special task that has to be solved by pregnancy and becoming a mother lies within the sphere of distribution and shifts between the cathexis of self representation and object representation.' For some women, pregnancy may be one of the most enriching stages of the life cycle, for when is one nearer to feeling like God than when creating a new life? In this way, for a young woman whose experience with her own mother has been 'good enough', the temporary regression to a primary identification with the omnipotent, fertile, life-giving mother, as well as with herself as if she were her own child, is a pleasurable developmental phase in which further maturation and growth of the self may be achieved. For other women, the inevitable regression occasioned by pregnancy and motherhood may be a painful and frightening experience. The infantile wish to merge with the mother and the opposing fear of it which occasioned a partial failure of self/object differentiation may be revived. In this way, fantasies about the primary unity of mother and baby cannot be successfully integrated with adult reality, where such differentiation is paramount.

The Infantile Wish to Have a Child

Childhood wishes to identify with a primary object, the powerful pre-oedipal mother, are foreshadowed in play and fantasy long before there is any possibility of parenthood (Deutsch, 1944; Benedek, 1959). Gender identity is established in early childhood, and sexual identity is largely resolved by the end of adolescence. Physiological maturation of the body forces an important stage of emotional separation–individuation upon the adolescent. Genital sexuality drives the adolescent towards the first intercourse, which confirms her right to own her body. There remains the later stage of parenthood to negotiate. First pregnancy affords a woman a further stage of identification rooted in a biological basis. She enters upon the final stage of being like her own mother, a physiologically mature woman, impregnated by her sexual partner – and in fantasy with her mother's – powerful enough to create life herself. It follows that the physical changes of pregnancy facilitate a woman's bodily re-experience of primary unity with her mother, and at the same time afford an experience of differentiation from her mother's body, which once contained her own. A further stage of separation–individuation is forced upon her.

Such bodily changes are inevitably accompanied by a re-enactment of infantile emotional development. The young woman may become aware of primitive, previously repressed fantasies and conflicts, arising from childhood sexual theories about her own conception, intrauterine life, and birth (Pines, 1972). It follows that positive and negative aspects of the self and of the object may be projected on to the unseen foetus as if it were an extension of them.

The unique combination of bodily and emotional feelings occasioned by first pregnancy affords a young woman an alternative means of resolving psychic conflict. The foetus may be physically retained, cocooned and given life, or it may be physically rejected, as in miscarriage or abortion, when the mother may deny the foetus life and deny motherhood to herself. In this way, the body may again be used to express emotional states of mind, as it was in earlier stages of infantile development. The little girl's fantasies of foetal survival concerning her siblings or herself may reinforce her feelings of omnipotence or helplessness. Such reactions are founded not only on early experiences of childhood and parenting but also on the family romance regarding the children's birth. If the little girl has been told of her mother's ambivalent feelings about her own conception it must, in my view, complicate her final identification, and make her ambivalent about pregnancy in her turn.

Use of the Body as an Alternative Means of Achieving Separation–Individuation

I shall now focus on the young woman's relationship to her body, to her self, to her own mother as an object, and to her experience of being physically and emotionally mothered. The mother is to her child the symbol both of the maturational environment and of motherliness itself. Her physical presence and emotional attitudes towards her child and its body are integrated with the child's experience and her conscious and unconscious fantasies. The representation of an internal mother created in this way is a lifelong model for her daughter to identify with and also to differentiate herself from.

It is generally agreed that the foundations of the self and the distinction between self and object are shaped by an integration of bodily experience with mental representation. It is only in early childhood that the little girl can begin not only to identify with her mother but also to introject a mutual feeling of bodily satisfaction between her mother and herself (E. Balint, 1973). I would add that if the little girl has not felt satisfied by her mother at the pre-oedipal stage, nor felt that she herself has satisfied her, she can never make up for this basic loss of a primary stable sense of well-being in her body and with her body image unless she sacrifices her normal drive towards a positive oedipal outcome (Pines, 1980). Narcissistic injury, giving rise to narcissistic rage, envy of the mother and lack of self-esteem, may be painful and add to the difficulties of separation.

The child's separation–individuation is influenced by the mother's capacity to enjoy her own adult sexual body and her relationship to the father. If she is satisfied in her own life, the psychologically symbiotic stage of her infant's life is not unduly prolonged, and the atmosphere of mutual pleasure between the parents, the mother's own enjoyment of her body and of her self, not only offer the child a satisfying object to internalize and identify with but also give her hope of achieving such a destiny herself.

It follows that a mother who is not satisfied with herself as a woman, and cannot accept the father as a man, has difficulty in separating from the child in whom she hopes to find all that she herself has missed, and through whom she wants to live again. Fantasy and reality become blurred for the mother if the fusion and symbiosis of pregnancy are not psychologically severed. Fantasy and reality become blurred for the child if the mother's behaviour is not experienced as good-enough adaptive mothering in which good and bad are integrated rather than split. This leads to difficulties of separation for mother and child alike. Does the child experience her body and later her thoughts and her fantasies as being clearly her own, or are they still confused with her mother's, as her body was in the primitive, symbiotic stages preceding self and object differentiation?

Biological puberty necessitates a change of body image from that of a child to that of an adult woman capable of bearing a child herself. The girl's awareness of her developing adult body not only revives previous conflicts about her identification with her mother but also intensifies bodily feelings and stimulation. There is an upsurge of emotional regressive tendencies as well as a thrust towards maturation, and a compromise between these two must be achieved. A young woman's physiologically mature and sexually alive body establishes adult status but also enables her to split off and deny painful emotional states by substituting bodily sensations. In this way, feelings of love or hate towards the self or towards the object can be concretely expressed, depression avoided and self-esteem raised. It follows that a sexual act which, to the outside world, appears to be an act of adult, genital sexuality, may unconsciously become a means of satisfying unfulfilled pre-genital longings for the mother and for being mothered.

In my experience, adolescent girls who precociously embark on heterosexual relationships are using their bodies to re-experience the most primitive contact between mother and child. Foreplay is satisfying, but they are usually frigid on penetration. In this way, they attempt to establish an object relationship which will compensate for an earlier lack of internalization of a satisfied and satisfactory mother–child relationship – an attempt that is doomed to failure, since physical penetration or emotional involvement with a sexual partner reactivates the primitive anxieties of merging or annihilation of the self which the mother–infant relationship originally evoked. What has not been achieved in these girls is growth towards a more mature identification with the mother's adult alive and sexual body, capable of sexual response to penetration by the father and of being impregnated by him. Nor are they able to value their sexual partners or other objects as real people with emotional needs, since all they seek is a return to the infantile omnipotence of the baby. Physical maturation, well-trained intelligence, and worldly success may not affect or influence the regressive fixation of this aspect of emotional growth to an infantile stage. Mature object love, in which the needs of self and object are mutually understood and fulfilled, cannot be achieved, and the birth of a real baby might be a calamity.

Clinical Material

Mrs X was a thirty-six-year-old white teacher who sought help for a severe depression. She had a broken marriage and numerous affairs with black partners behind her. She had longed to be a writer but had become intellectually blocked during her university training, so she had become a teacher and professional literary critic instead. She had always been interested in dreams and dreaming. In the first few sessions of the analysis, it became clear that her depression had begun nine months after she had had her last abortion, resulting from her relationship with her current black lover. She had consciously planned it, with no hesitation or apparent guilt, since she came from a country where sexual relations between people of different races were forbidden. A black child would not have been tolerated by anyone, especially her own mother. After this event, Mrs X left her current job and came to this country with her lover, who had cared for her and treated her very tenderly after the abortion, as if she herself were the lost baby. Mrs X enjoyed the dependence upon him as if she were the baby and he the parent, until the moment when her baby would have been born and she would have had to assume the maternal role herself.

Mrs X was the elder of two intelligent and attractive daughters. Her father, a passive and retiring man, had died of carcinoma of the penis after a long hospitalization when she was fifteen years old. Her mother was a vigorous, attractive woman who had married her lover immediately after her husband's death. Before he died, Mrs X's father told her that he had left her some money to go to college, and she had been guiltily aware of her wish that her father should die sooner than he did, since his prolonged suffering was distressing for the whole family. After his death, Mrs X's mother told her that no money was available for her education, but it was quite obvious that there was plenty of money for other expenses she considered more essential, such as clothes and make-up to enhance her daughter's physical appearance, just as she used her money to enhance her own.

This was but one incident in a lifelong situation in which Mrs X's separate emotional needs and ambitions had not been acknowledged by her mother, although she had always cared for her body. Mrs X had always felt that her attractive body and appearance had never satisfied her mother but had been used by her as an extension of her own in order to attract men. Mrs X's mother frequently told her that she had never been sexually satisfied by her father, and Mrs X felt that it had followed that she had never satisfied her mother either. She was aware of her mother's secret assignations with lovers despite her father's illness, and was angered by his passive acceptance of this situation and of his impending death. The anger was never verbalized and she remained the good child, but began to fail academically because she felt confused and unable to think.

Adolescence enabled her to find an alternative way of dealing with her painful situation. By using her body she could bypass the painful affects of mourning her father's loss and the narcissistic rage that her mother's involvement with her lover evoked in her. Her body also enabled her to regain the regressive, primitive satisfaction of the mother–baby relationship in which she sought comfort, since her mother could not comfort her in any way. Mrs X's mother was angry at her daughter's attempts to separate from her, and made her guilty in return. Eventually, the situation became so intolerable that Mrs X made an abortive suicide attempt. The policeman who saved her and took her back to her mother reprimanded her severely and told her that she was her mother's property until she was eighteen, and had no right to kill herself. This confirmed her conviction that her body was her mother's, not her own.

A dream and its associations later in the analysis helped us to understand her dilemma. In the dream, Mrs X was crying and turned to her lover for comfort. In response, he came towards her and removed a false white front and offered her his black breast to suck. But the male breast gave no milk and Mrs X was left hungry and desperate. Following the working-through of the dream, and the subsequent material, Mrs X recognized that in every man she was looking for her mother, and that even in someone who was physically so different, the relationship was basically a repetition of the emotionally uncomfortable one she had had with her own mother in which she felt she was clinging on to someone who could deny her life and food, as in the dream, at any minute. The dream marked a moment of insight in which she had to recognize that she longed for the maternal breast which she could never find again.

Mrs X's relationship with her mother had been uneven; symbiotic and mutually satisfying in the beginning but stormy as soon as Mrs X, as a child, tried to move away and become emotionally separate. At any move she made, her mother was enraged, demanding and authoritarian. She told Mrs X repeatedly what a bad child she was, and angrily told her that even in the womb she had defied her and that she had, in fact, tried to abort her during pregnancy. Mrs X was never openly angry with her mother, although she was provocative, but was left with an image of herself as a bad child and a representation of her mother as a potentially murderous figure.

Mrs X's relationships with men followed a similar pattern. They had always been stormy, and she provoked the men to violent anger, although she herself showed none and remained the victim. The relationships were always brought to an end, mainly by Mrs X herself. In this way, she was in fantasy not only the baby who has to cling on to keep alive but also the mother who has to abort the foetus in her turn. The fantasy of clinging to life in spite of her powerful mother's attempts to abort her had been the basis of a narcissistic omnipotent fantasy which she acted out by making life-and-death decisions for the foetus.

After this dream, Mrs X disclosed that she had had three planned abortions during her adult life, each time becoming pregnant by a man whom she seduced into the relationship. None of the men wanted children. Shortly after aborting the foetus she aborted the relationship with the man, just as she had had two previous attempts at therapy which each time she had also aborted. What also emerged during her analysis was that emotional closeness in which she sought and regained the earliest pleasure of the symbiotic, mutually satisfying relationship with her mother also revived primitive fears of merging, since her mother could not recognize her as an emotionally separate being with needs of her own, or let her separate in her turn. Pregnancy was therefore, for Mrs X, a concrete proof that she owned her own body and was a woman in her own right; but emotional separation from her mother was not achieved. If the foetus grew and became a baby who would be fed at her breast, she could never emotionally be a baby again, and this she could not tolerate. The infant's omnipotence and merging with the mother was what she longed to return to. Once her sexual identity and separateness from her mother's body had been concretely established by pregnancy, she could abort the foetus as if it were a meaningless part of herself. Yet Mrs X remembered the dates at which these babies might have been born, and how old they would have been.

What became meaningful in the course of her analysis was Mrs X's use of her body to seek revenge on her dominating mother. Her sexuality was enjoyed with men her mother disapproved of, and she gave her no grandchild to replace herself. We understood that in this way – by aborting the foetus, her relationships and her previous attempts at analysis – Mrs X had felt herself to be even more grandiose and omnipotent than the bad and murderous aggressor-mother with whom she was identified. The foetus also represented herself as the unwanted, difficult child her mother had said she was, and the murderous aggressor-mother. There was no viable alternative to identification with a bad mother and a bad child.

This was subtly reflected in the transference. Mrs X had been referred to me by a colleague in her own country. When I first saw her I did not have a vacancy and wanted to refer her to a colleague. As soon as I had told her this, Mrs X, despite her distress, insisted that she could work only with me and would wait. Shortly, I had an unexpected vacancy and we began to work together. What Mrs X had undoubtedly understood in the first interview was my interest in the narrative of her first pregnancy and abortion, since pregnancy had been a special area for my analytic interest. My difficulty in finding her a vacancy and her persistence in waiting for me had been a transference manifestation of her basic omnipotent fantasy of clinging to an ambivalent mother and seducing her into giving her life.

Mrs X attempted from the first to establish an ambivalent countertransference in which we would re-enact a sadomasochistic relationship. Payments of fees were frequently in arrears, and holiday breaks were never adhered to by her. This was her attempt to make me into a greedy, demanding, angry figure who would make her guilty at having a separate existence. Mrs X could not lie on the couch but brought many dreams, which at this stage were prolific and colourful. She wrote them all in a notebook which she brought to each session, but what was striking was the little-girl affectless voice in which she read them to me. She also interpreted the dreams very cleverly, leaving me no room for my own creativity as an analyst. My role was to be the admiring spectator of her cleverness and her ability to control the whole situation by being both analyst and patient. This was a re-enactment of her family romance. She had been the admired first child and grandchild. Her mother had often told her that she had considered her, as a baby, cleverer than herself. In this way, the childhood situation of omnipotence and helplessness was repeated. The cleverness of the baby was used to disguise the feelings of anxiety at the beginning of analysis. The dreams were good and fruitful products, but she could not risk my interpretations lest they prove to be critical attacks which would fragment her precarious sense of self.

Once she had tested my capacity to be patient, to contain and tolerate this situation, without becoming the destructive and controlling parental figure that she wanted me to be and yet hoped I would not be, Mrs X could lie on the couch and allow herself to regress in the analytic situation. Numerous instances of her lover's controlling and often sadistic behaviour were related to me in an affectless voice while I silently experienced feelings of outrage and pity for her as the helpless victim of his cruelty, and wondered how she could survive. It was as if we were together repeating a primitive psychological symbiotic stage of the mother–infant relationship in which the baby's non-verbal experiences are mediated not only by the mother's response to that infant, but also by her own past history and current life. In this way, my countertransference – based on my response to my patient, but also on my own life – was to be the most subtle tool available for Mrs X's analysis.

Following our understanding of the analytic situation,

much of the subsequent work was centred upon Mrs X's need to remain in a state of emotional fusion with her mother, despite her opposing wish to be separate and free. Since childhood she had related all her problems with her parents to friends and acted according to their reactions of indignation on her behalf, since she had no way of judging for herself. She said, 'I feel as if the central core of my self is missing.' We understood that the inability to remain pregnant was a symptom of deeper feelings of the need to remain empty and dead.

As the therapeutic alliance developed, Mrs X began to be more in touch with her own feelings. She was now frightened of her own dreams, since she allowed me to interpret them in order to be helped; but the loss of control and infantile omnipotence was difficult to bear, as was our deepening closeness. Her depression and sadness – not only about the loss of her position as the clever baby both in the analysis and with her lover, but also about the loss of her professional identity, as the clever critic, her mother – was verbalized, and enabled her to be sad also about the loss of the last pregnancy. But it was curious that she expressed no guilt about it. Nevertheless, every session in which we understood each other and insight was deepened was immediately followed by a negative therapeutic reaction or by the intensification of the sado-masochistic aspects of her relationship with her lover. It was as if the establishment of a satisfying and satisfactory relationship between us was both too pleasurable and too threatening.

Interpretations that showed understanding aroused Mrs X's fears of fusion with me, and she again used her body in order to separate us by having intercourse with her lover before every analytic hour. In this way, the excitement of good emotional closeness with me and the fear of merging were diffused by a physical experience of orgiastic fusion with a man. We now understood that on a deeper level every man was provoked by Mrs X's tales into hating her mother and separating them. Her sexual affairs with black men were to use her body as if it were an extension of her mother's, and subtly to humiliate her in this way. Mrs X's mother frequently criticized her and reproached her, saying, 'How can your body, which was once in mine, feel anything for a man I cannot tolerate!' In this way, we could see that Mrs X's mother shared her daughter's fantasy of owning her body and of fusion with her. Mrs X's fears of her mother's envy of her were also avoided by her choice of a man she could not envy. This was a re-enactment of her intense childhood envy of her attractive mother, repeated in her adolescence, and seen in the transference in her envious attacks upon our work together. We were not to be mutually satisfied and excited by the creation of a living experience together, but to conceive a child which Mrs X would then abort. This was reflected in Mrs X's own creativity, where she could create exciting and lively ideas for her students to execute but could not sustain them herself. In this way, her inability to produce a live baby was complemented by her inability to write, since she projected her destructive wishes on to the outside world in which every reader was the critical, sadistic mother with whom she felt fused.

Our analytic work was now focused upon the projection of sadistic impulses on to her mother in the first instance and on to her analyst in the transference. Mrs X could now begin to accept her own sadism. She said, 'I do what my mother only wanted to do.' Later she wept, saying, 'I murdered those babies.' Interpretation of Mrs X's inability to accept the good mother in her analyst, her mother or herself led her to reveal a fantasy which had secretly predominated her childhood and had never been repressed. In the fantasy there had never been a time

111

when she had not existed. She had always been an egg hiding in her mother's womb, waiting to be fertilized by her father's sperm. By means of this fantasy she had been part of the parental intercourse at her own conception. It followed that in fantasy she had not only caused the cancer of the penis from which her father died by biting his penis when he penetrated – mouth and vagina being indistinguishable – but the primary fusion of mother and child was maintained, in which it was not clear whether she was her own mother or herself. Any pregnancy of her own was thus in danger of fulfilling the oedipal wish which had not been repressed. The fertilized egg, the foetus that was inside her, could be concretely expelled without guilt, since it represented both the dangerous cancer that had killed her father and the sadistic aspects of herself fused with those that she had projected into her mother.

We could now see the calamity that faced her if she felt better in analysis. If she could accept her parents as good and capable of satisfying each other, just as she would have to accept her analyst and herself as being good and capable of a satisfying relationship, then she would have to face an overwhelming sense of guilt at having in an omnipotent fantasy destroyed their marriage; and it followed that in her omnipotent fantasy she also destroyed her own analysis. The price she paid for this sadistic fantasy, which was never suppressed, was heavy in her life. She could struggle for the fulfilment of her conscious wish to achieve an adult relationship, a mature biological feminine identity, an academic success, but would deny herself fulfilment of these aims. She could survive, but not grant herself a licence to live, since she felt her mother had never done so.

It became clear that the unrepressed incestuous sexual fantasy of the earlier pre-oedipal phase and of the oedipal phase had dominated Mrs X's life. The sadistic pleasure contained in this powerful fantasy, and in her pleasure at having defeated her mother in the womb and given her pain, drove her to choose not only black sexual partners, physically unlike her father, but also those who did not want children. In this way, she solved her ambivalent wishes by relying on their views. Thus she could abort the unborn child who also represented the hidden oedipal partner, the dead cancerous father whom she could destroy again. A dream, and its associations following analysis of this material, revealed another aspect of her dilemma. After our mutual decision to terminate the analysis in a year's time since Mrs X had to return to her own country, she dreamed that she had decided to have an abortion. It had been noteworthy that she had neither wished to become pregnant nor wished to have an abortion now except in her dream. In the dream, after the abortion the doctor showed her the foetus and gave her some of his own blood for the paternity test. It looked painful, but the doctor did it to help her. In her associations it emerged that the foetus was a cancer, a representation of the father inside her whom she could not mourn and let go. No sexual partner could replace him, since emotional separation from him would confirm his destruction, just as separation from her mother was unconsciously equated with her death. The foetus that could be destroyed by abortion and replaced by a new pregnancy was a concrete bodily representation of both parents, whom she both loved and hated. In thinking about her father's death, from this point in her analysis, Mrs X realized that she had thought he had never separated from his own mother and that in her fantasy his death was equated with a return to the womb. In this way, death and intrauterine life before birth were unconsciously equated.

Analysis has allowed Mrs X to mourn for her dead father. Previously repressed memories of the good times between her parents and herself have emerged. She is beginning to write again; she was helped to do this by recalling the memory of her dead father as a loving parent who cared for her, and it was as if she were writing for him. She has achieved a more mature relationship with her mother and has been able to say to her, 'If my father had lived, my life would have been different', and her mother has, for the first time also allowed herself to cry for her first husband. They have since shared grief and mourning for the death of the mother's second husband. Mrs X dreams of pregnancy and abortion, but no longer has to act it out. She is wondering whether to continue with her unsatisfying relationship with her lover, or separate from him and fulfil herself in her own right. She has met a man with whom she feels she could have a more suitable relationship. The acceptance of her own sadistic wishes, as well as her loving feelings and the mourning for her father, has offered her a choice of living or surviving.

Conclusion

The conclusions that form the final part of this paper are drawn not only from the analysis of Mrs X but also from my clinical experience with other women patients. First pregnancy is an important developmental phase in a woman's lifelong task of separation–individuation from her own mother. To be pregnant offers a woman a further stage of emotional identification with the pre-oedipal mother, based on a biological foundation. The experience of a child inside her own body also enables a woman to differentiate her body from that of her mother, whence she herself came. The concrete physical experience of symbiosis between the mother and the foetus now inside

114

her adult body is paralleled by an emotional symbiosis. Mother and child at this stage are felt to be a self-object. A woman, pregnant for the first time, has to achieve a new adaptive position within both her inner world and the outer object world. The internal identifications with her own mother as the object and the narcissistic identification with the foetus as if it were herself are heightened by the normal regression experienced in pregnancy.

Maternal pre-conceptive ambivalence, if it is known to the little girl, may distort the outcome of a young woman's first pregnancy, since the biological basis for identification with her own mother is now achieved for the first time. The foetus inside her body now represents good and bad aspects of the self and of the object, and the mother may not give it a licence to live if she herself feels that she has never been granted one by her own mother. The pregnant mother's ambivalence towards her unborn child may reflect earlier intense ambivalent feelings towards her own mother, resulting in a difficulty in self-object differentiation and further difficulty in separation–individuation. A weak relationship with an undemonstrative father does not help the child to separate from the mother or to view herself as a child loved and wanted by both parents and endowed with a life of her own. A pervasive sense of guilt at being alive despite her mother's pre-conceptive ambivalence may give rise to problems in living to the full, since the child may feel she has a licence only to survive. Pride in survival despite the powerful, murderous aggressor-mother may also be a source of omnipotent fantasies for the child and a justification for sadistic fantasies re-enacted in wider object relationships. Separation is unconsciously equated with death of the self or the object. Difficulties in accepting the mother as a good mother may lead to a woman's difficulties in accepting the creative and life-giving aspects of herself.

PREGNANCY, MISCARRIAGE AND ABORTION*

Despite a growing interest in the psychoanalytic understanding of pregnancy, there is as yet no literature on spontaneous abortion or miscarriage, although some attention has been paid to planned abortion. Analysis of women patients who have miscarried[1] often reveals, many years after this event, their sense of loss, prolonged grief and unresolved mourning – a longstanding depression, a loss of self-esteem and a hatred of their female bodies which do not bear live children as their mothers did. Their self-representation is damaged.

Here I shall discuss miscarriage – that is, spontaneous abortion – and planned abortion, their psychological

---

* Presented at the 36th International Psychoanalytical Congress, Rome, August 1989, and published in *International Journal of Psycho-Analysis* (1990) 71: 301–7.

antecedents and consequences. In both situations young women become pregnant, enter a normal further developmental stage of the life cycle, but are unable to continue their pregnancy to become mothers and bring a live child into the world. Thus spontaneous abortion is frequently a threat to normal first pregnancy. The medical reasons are often difficult to diagnose and treat, and do not necessarily recur in subsequent pregnancies. Most miscarriages occur during the first trimester of pregnancy, when the woman consciously experiences the developing foetus as an integral part of herself. Her dreams may reveal other aspects of unconscious fantasy and anxiety, such as who does the foetus represent, and who has fathered the oedipal girl's baby in a forbidden guilt-laden intercourse.

In analysing women's dreams I have been impressed by the influence of physiological bodily changes on psychic life. Dreams may reflect a woman's bodily hormonal change during a menstrual cycle. Mind and bodily changes influence each other in a woman's monthly and developmental cycle, and the intimate link between them allows a woman unconsciously to use her body in an attempt to avoid psychic conflict. In considering women patients in my practice who have had miscarriages, I have come to speculate on some possible unconscious reasons for some spontaneous abortions. Psychoanalysis, in which the patient's unconscious reasons for miscarriage become conscious, may help her to retain the foetus during pregnancy and give birth to a live child.

A first pregnancy, a move from childlessness towards parenthood, is a time of emotional and psychological upheaval. Yet it is a normal developmental phase despite the emotional crisis it provokes, and a valuable time of emotional preparation for motherhood. During pregnancy, particularly first pregnancy, conflicts belonging to past developmental stages are revived, and the young woman has to deal with them in a new way, internally and externally. We may therefore view first pregnancy as a crisis point in the long search for a feminine identity, and as a point of no return.

Pregnancy is an important phase in a woman's life-long task of separation and individuation from her own mother (Pines, 1982). As we saw in Chapter 6, 'The Relevance of Early Psychic Development to Pregnancy and Abortion', childhood wishes to identify with a pri-mary object – the powerful pre-oedipal mother – can be seen in play and fantasy long before there is any possibility of parenthood.

When, in adolescence, a young girl embarks on her own sexual life, she confirms her rights and responsibili-ties over her own body, separate from her mother's. Her mother's ownership of her daughter's body has now ceased. However, pregnancy enables her to re-experience a feeling of primary unity with her mother and at the same time to identify narcissistically with the intrauterine foetus, as if it were herself in her mother's body. Such a symbiotic state in the future mother may activate intense ambivalent feelings towards both the foetus and her own mother. For a young woman who has had a good experi-ence with her own mother, the temporary regression to a primary identification with a generous life-giving mother as well as with herself, as if she were her own infant, is a pleasurable developmental phase. For others, where am-bivalent feelings towards the mother have been unresolved or negative feelings towards the self, the sexual partner or important figures from the past predominate, the inevi-table regressions of pregnancy facilitate the projection of such feelings on to the foetus. Thus the foetus may already possess a negative prenatal identity in the mother's mind long before the birth.

In a first pregnancy, the young woman has two alternative means of resolving psychic conflict. The foetus may be safely held inside her and allowed to grow and flourish from month to month, or it may be physically rejected, as in miscarriage and abortion. A mother may thus either facilitate life and motherhood or destroy them both. Unfulfilled pregnancy and the failure to produce a live child – because of unconscious reasons for spontaneous abortion or conscious reasons for planned abortion – will affect each patient individually. Interaction between fantasy and reality in the pregnant woman's mind will influence the emotional outcome. Some women, as soon as they know they are pregnant, have in conscious fantasy and daydreams, or in unconscious fantasy and night dreams, the picture of an actual baby in their minds, sometimes even with a sexual identity of its own. These women look forward to becoming good-enough mothers, as they experienced their own mothers. Miscarriage for them is a painful loss, as if a full-term baby had died and had to be mourned.

Other women regard the foetus as a part of their body which can simply be dispensed with. Their conscious wish to become pregnant does not have motherhood as its ultimate goal. Pregnancy for them may be an unconscious means of confirming a female sexual identity or adult physical maturity. The foetus is not represented in fantasy, dreams or reality as a baby, but rather as an aspect of the bad self, or as a bad internal object that must be expelled. Analysis of such patients reveals an early relationship with the mother which is suffused with frustration, rage, disappointment and guilt. Loss of the foetus, by either miscarriage or abortion, is experienced as a relief rather than a loss, as if the continuing internal bad mother had not given permission for the child to become a mother herself. It is possible that the pregnant woman's unconscious anxieties connected with the fantasy of the

119

foetus, representing a bad and dangerous aspect of the self or of her partner, may be a contributing factor to the stimulation of uterine expulsive movements, which end in miscarriage. The analyst is experienced as this malign internal mother in the transference. Analysis of these aspects of psychic life may enable a woman to maintain her pregnancy and become a mother herself.

Freud's predominant attitude towards motherhood was that the mother's first child was the extension of her own narcissism; thus her ambivalence towards her living child would be positively resolved. Her child would feel wanted and loved. Her love for this living child would elicit guilt about her negative feelings and prompt her towards reparation. However, Freud also acknowledged maternal ambivalence and the difficulty for a mother in having a surviving yet unwanted child. 'How many mothers who love their children tenderly, perhaps over-tenderly, conceived them unwillingly and wished at the time that the living thing within them might not develop further?' (Freud, 1916–17).

Clinical experience leads us to recognize that ambivalence, whether latent or manifest, is present in all parent–child relationships, and much depends on the relationship between the biological parents, and their attitude to their future child. The biblical myth of Moses, the Greek myth of Oedipus and the Celtic legend of Merlin, all babies abandoned by the parents after their birth, illustrate the universality of this theme. Clinical experience bears out the universality of the temptation to be physically or emotionally cruel to a helpless, demanding baby or to a difficult, growing child. This universal parental dilemma may be highlighted in our countertransference feelings when a patient's behaviour may oppose our personal standards of morality. In these circumstances, particularly with perverse or sadistic patients, the neutral stance of the analyst may be particularly difficult to maintain. The analyst may have to monitor her own position in order to withstand the temptation to take on the role of the parent who judges and maintains standards of morality for the recalcitrant child.

I shall try to illustrate my view regarding the universal dilemma of maternal ambivalence and its varying solutions by introducing material from three patients. The first patient was a victim of the Holocaust, and her traumatic experiences led her to miscarry several times. The second patient had an extremely difficult relationship with her own mother; despite a conscious wish to have a child, analysis revealed her unconscious ambivalence towards the foetus, but also helped her not to miscarry. The third patient had intentionally aborted three pregnancies and felt relieved when her menopause approached and she could no longer be pregnant.

Clinical Illustration 1

Mrs A was a survivor of the Holocaust. One week after her first period had started, she was sent to Auschwitz. Her parents perished there. After her release from the camp, Mrs A emigrated to England and married. Her periods returned irregularly. Mrs A longed to become pregnant and bring a new life into her new world which was no longer dominated by sadism and physical death. For her, as for many survivors of the Holocaust, babies represented the restoration of normality from a psychotic world and the re-establishment of family life. Unconsciously, Mrs A's future children were to replace her dead parents. Mrs A, who was so desperate to have a child, joyfully became pregnant several times, but every time she miscarried. Each miscarriage was physically unbearable. She took a long time to recover physically, and

121

frequently remained huddled under her bedcovers in a darkened room.

Mrs A was living in her present reality, as well as in the past reality of Auschwitz, where she had spent so much time hiding under her ragged bedcovers. Her past had not been integrated, and mourning for the murdered past objects had not been achieved. Two vital aspects of emotional identification in pregnancy were impossible for her: identification with her own mother and identification with the foetus as if it were herself. Although Mrs A had seen her dead mother's body, she could not let her die in her mind and thus mourn her, for that involved her own guilt at surviving her. Identification with the foetus as a representation of herself was too traumatic to bear. Her wish to become pregnant also contained her unconscious wish for rebirth, and for a new self, yet there was no viable alternative in her mind to a murdered mother and a traumatized child. Thus, while pregnancy satisfied her wish to become a mother, miscarriage enabled her to avoid her own mother's fate and spared her unborn child from the fate that had been her own. Analysis enabled Mrs A to begin mourning her past and to fight for her right to emotional survival. Her acceptance of her analyst as a strong, life-giving mother in the transference encouraged her to bring new life into a safer world. Mrs A eventually had a family of three children, although she never forgot the age that the miscarried babies might have been had they survived.

Clinical Illustration 2

Mrs B had married late in life, and consciously longed to fulfil her childhood wish to have a child in the short time that was available to her before the menopause. She was the only daughter of a professional woman who devalued her own femininity and that of her little girl. Mrs B's mother doted on her two elder sons and constantly praised their physical and academic achievements, while Mrs B's own achievements appeared to her to remain unnoticed. Mrs B's father was ill and retiring, so that the mother's identification with her sons influenced the solution of her daughter's oedipal conflict. Mrs B knew she wanted to be a boy throughout her childhood in order to gain her mother's love, as her brothers had done. Her quick intelligence enabled her to achieve high academic rewards, which eventually won her mother's admiration, but Mrs B's femininity and pleasure in her female body remained unsatisfying to her, since her mother had valued neither her daughter's femininity nor her own. For several childhood years, however, a secret relationship with her younger brother, consisting of mutual masturbation, had enabled her to enjoy giving and receiving sexual pleasure with a male, which raised her self-esteem. Nevertheless, the underlying difficult early relationship with her mother, in which she felt that neither of them was satisfying or satisfactory to the other, led to an unstable basic sense of well-being and narcissistic difficulties, which Mrs B attempted to solve by a series of heterosexual relationships. These were physically satisfying but emotionally painful. Her first lover was old and gentle, as her father had been; those who succeeded him were younger and treated her badly and scornfully, as her brothers had done.

During the course of her analysis, Mrs B's initial transference feelings towards her female analyst – originally seen as the projected terrifying powerful mother of her internal world who could neither give nor receive love – were modified. A warmer and easier relationship with both her mother and her analyst ensued. Mrs B, now more capable of giving and receiving love, found a caring partner. She married him and became pregnant. Consciously she was delighted, yet it became clear as the pregnancy progressed that she remained unconsciously ambivalent towards her future child. She did not look after her own health, nor that of her foetus, which the scan had revealed was a boy. The earlier conflicts and difficulties that appeared to have been previously worked through in her analysis re-emerged during her pregnancy, as if the new identity of future mother to a child threatened her old identity. Her mother showed no enthusiasm for her daughter's pregnancy. Mrs B bled, but would not rest in order to save her baby. A dream, after a short break when I cancelled three sessions, revealed her conflict. In the dream she was walking with her mother and felt that she was in danger of miscarrying. Her mother said nothing could be done, but Mrs B knew that she must hurry to the hospital, where the doctor would save her baby. Her mother said there was no point, and did not help her or give her permission to bear a living baby. Mrs B knew that the hospital doctor represented her analyst, whose positive response to her pregnancy reinforced her husband's confirmation of herself as a woman. Analysis had shown her that something could be done in the past, and she was impatiently waiting for her analyst to return. Mrs B did not in fact miscarry.

As her pregnancy proceeded and the reality of the kicking baby inside her impelled her towards her new identity, a series of dreams revealed the compelling re-emergence of her analytic themes. In the first dream she was applying for a new passport; in another she was at a swimming pool where the big boys were rough with a little boy and pushed him under the water. Another woman jumped in and saved him, and Mrs B was relieved to see that he was alive. In her associations Mrs B remembered being pushed underwater by her brothers; a

124

woman nearby had shouted and made them stop. She was dismayed that even in her dream it had to be her analyst who saved the boy foetus and not herself, as if she was identified with the mother who did not save her. She was relieved that her ambivalence could be calmly accepted by her analyst, her unconscious guilt made conscious and her pregnancy kept safe. In other dreams Mrs B's childhood envy of her brothers came to the fore. She dreamt that she was a hermaphrodite and allowed herself to remember that as a small girl she had thought of herself as a brain-damaged small boy. This new material enabled a further working-through of her ambivalence towards boys, and towards her unborn baby boy. Finally it became clear that for her the unseen foetus was an oedipal child, and thus evidence of her fantasied incestuous relationship with her brother. Resolution of so much unconscious guilt during the course of her pregnancy has helped Mrs B to become a good mother to her baby boy, with whom she is closely identified.

Case Illustration 3

My final case illustration concerns a young woman who could not completely master the developmental phase of passing from adolescence to young adulthood. Despite her marriage to a young man whom she loved, Mrs C had difficulty in emotionally separating from her own mother and taking responsibility for her separate existence, her own body, and her sexuality. Analysis revealed that her present difficulties had started in childhood, when she experienced difficulty in accepting her femininity and her female body. Since Mrs C's thinking was blocked by long-standing infantile rage and frustration which her parents did not allow her to express, as well as by her guilt about infantile sexuality, with its repressed bodily excitement and sexual fantasies, her emotional problems were unconsciously acted out by means of her body. Mrs C had had three abortions before her marriage, and one attempt at analysis which was aborted by her husband's unexpected professional move to London, before she came to see me.

Mrs C came from a Catholic family in South America and was educated in a strict Catholic school administered by nuns. There she had been taught that sexuality was for reproduction, not pleasure. This teaching made it impossible for her to use contraception when she became an adult woman. She was also influenced by the family legend that her parents had fallen in love at first sight and lived happily ever after. In the little girl's fantasy their sexual life had begun after marriage, when their four children were conceived. She had been told by her mother that they wanted children to complete their happiness. Mrs C was the youngest child and the only girl, and her female body was strictly controlled by her mother. When she was a baby, feeding times were regulated strictly by the clock rather than by the infant's bodily needs, and early toilet training was imposed upon her.

She was a sulky, defiant little girl until eventually her exasperated parents threatened to send her to a boarding school. Thereafter she became compliant and good. She expressed some of her rebelliousness and anger by keeping her room in a terrible mess. Her father was angered by this behaviour, which was understood in the analysis as guilty provocation for him to punish her for her repressed anger, but the numerous maids in the household quickly cleaned up before he came home so that the unconscious wish for punishment was always revived but never fulfilled. The untidy room was symbolic of Mrs C's untidy mind, in which there was no room for her own thoughts, which had been split off and repressed, only for her mother's.

Mrs C's mother continued to control her daughter's body and appearance by dressing her as she thought appropriate, and filled her mind with strict rules of behaviour. However, she did not prepare her daughter for her first period. It came as a great shock and made her feel dirty and ashamed, as if once again she could not control her body sphincters, as had happened when she was a child and occasionally wet her bed. In puberty her body developed well before her friends' bodies.

Her growing breasts and secondary sexual characteristics, in a developing body whose growth she could not control, made her feel ashamed. She hid it; she would not wear a swimming costume, and she covered herself with a towel when she sat on the beach during the family holidays. She also became obstinately silent with her mother, thus not giving her rage utterance or allowing her mother's words to penetrate. She failed at school, and her bad self-image was overwhelming. The revival of sexuality – this time in an adult body – that adolescence initiates offered Mrs C an alternative way of restoring her self-esteem, now mirrored in the eyes of a persistent boyfriend who passionately pursued her. Through him she was able to see herself as an attractive girl rather than the messy girl she felt herself to be. Since she was unable to think for herself, and her Catholic education did not allow her to use contraceptives, Mrs C reciprocated his passion without consciously recognizing or thinking about the risks they were running. Unconsciously, she also expected him to be the adult and take responsibility for her and her body, as her mother had always done. Her pregnancy and subsequent abortion filled her with despair, since she had expected him to love her as her father was said to have loved her mother, and for the two of them to have lived happily ever after, as in her family romance. Sexual passion could be permitted only if it was idealized as romantic love.

Mrs C, though unconsciously sensing that her lover had no intention of taking responsibility for her or marrying her, resumed their relationship without either of them taking contraceptive precautions. She again became pregnant, and aborted the pregnancy. Later in her analysis we understood that her second pregnancy was a compulsive melancholic reparation for the first aborted one rather than a genuine wish to have a baby. It was also symbolic of the deeper psychic problems of taking adult responsibility for herself and her body, since she had no conscious thought of how she would take responsibility for a real baby. A woman's normal narcissistic identification with her own mother had pushed her forwards to achieving pregnancy, the final stage of bodily identification with her. Her own emotional developmental state, however, remained that of a dependent child. She could not emotionally trust herself to grow into a mature woman who would become a mother and take responsibility for a helpless dependent baby.

Mrs C's lover left her when he knew she was pregnant for the second time, and she felt she had no choice but to abort the pregnancy again. Following this she fell into a deep depression for which she was admitted to a hospital, where she regressed and lay in bed and was washed and fed as if she had become the baby herself. She recovered after the date at which the child would have been born. Although she was beautiful, Mrs C again felt ugly and unlovable until she met another young man who fell in love with her and this time wanted to marry her. Mirrored in his loving eyes, she felt admired and lovable. The date was fixed for a large Society wedding in her home town.

Yet again she made passionate and unprotected love with her future husband, became pregnant and aborted the foetus. It was as if she was compelled not only to become pregnant but also to abort. Thenceforward Mrs

C became depressed, and after her magnificent wedding the marriage became asexual, since she could not allow her husband to penetrate her. It remained so for several years. So she punished her husband and herself by not allowing them mutual sexual pleasure. It was as if she could define herself neither as an adult sexual woman nor as a good child. There was no viable alternative to aborting her bad dependent baby-self, but in doing so she also lost the good aspects of herself.

Mrs C began analysis with me with both of us consciously accepting the possibility that our joint work might be aborted by a further move abroad imposed by her husband's work. Unconsciously, it may have been possible for Mrs C to begin analysis and take the risk of engaging in a new relationship only if she knew she might not be trapped in it for ever. This undoubtedly reflected her dilemma in giving birth to a live child, since she feared feeling as trapped in the new relationship to the child as she felt trapped in her relationship to her mother, her husband and her new analyst.

At first Mrs C was as silent with me as she was with her mother and her husband. My interpretation that she could not allow me to penetrate her mind as her husband was not allowed to penetrate her body enabled her to begin talking. She comforted herself for the shame and humiliation of disclosing her thoughts by reminding herself that she paid me for analysis. Thus in the transference I became one of the maids who in her childhood had been paid to clear up her room. She began to talk of her shame that her body felt soiled by her abortions before her marriage after her dreams revealed her fear that her husband would abandon her, as her parents had once threatened to do. This again would have been her punishment, since she loved him and felt dependent on him. As this material was worked through, Mrs C's depression lifted, and she and her husband began to decorate their bedroom, which they had left unfinished until now. Nevertheless, her dreams continued to reveal her guilt about the improvement in her life, and her consequent and constant need to be punished. They also revealed her anxiety about the possibility of having to move abroad to a European city, which would interrupt her analysis.

One dream expressed her maturational growth in analysis, but also her fear of regression if she had to stop. Her own present furniture was being moved into her old room in her parents' house. She was afraid that if she went back to her own country she would again be trapped in her parents' house and unable to leave it to make her own life with her husband. She was afraid that her mother's depressive thoughts about a woman's life and anger towards men would again regulate her mind. However, she felt that she had grown in her analysis, and that she could now occupy her mind with her own thoughts, not her mother's. She felt guilty that she was so much happier while she was still aware of her mother's deep depression.

Mrs C recognized that she felt much closer to her husband, and that she was moving away from the sometimes undifferentiated relationship to her mother, in which she always felt that she was the dependent baby. This move was enacted in the transference when she began to speak English to me instead of her native language, which we had used before. So her feelings and thoughts were expressed in a new language mutually shared between us, not in her mother's. Now, in addition to her conflictual identification with her depressed and fragile mother, she saw in me a positive and independent woman with whom she could also identify.

Mrs C began to feel sexual desire for her husband, and actually allowed herself to think of the need for contraception. She consulted a gynaecologist. However, her earlier fear of bodily loss of control interfered with her sexuality, and again she could not allow her partner to penetrate. It was as if her adult self was again attacked by the dependent self who would have been punished for loss of sphincter control. Mrs C remembered that in her childhood – as we saw above – she had occasionally wet her bed, but the maids had helped her to avoid the punishment for soiling that her parents would have imposed. Thus the early difficulty of controlling her body sphincters in early childhood was repeated in adulthood. At this point her husband was posted to a city in Europe; this would indeed have aborted her analysis, but Mrs C thought about her situation and her loss, and decided to stay alone in London and go on with her analysis for some months. She commuted at weekends to join her husband and, despite her fears of being alone in their flat, continued our analytic work.

Mrs C felt deep pain about her abortions – that she had not been able to let her babies grow. She recognized her primitive omnipotence in deciding on life-and-death matters for the foetus. It seemed as if she felt that her mother had aborted her real self, and that she had functioned by means of a compliant false self which had covered an inner space empty of her real self. Throughout her life Mrs C had overeaten, because she had always felt so empty. She also recognized that in intercourse she controlled her husband's sexuality by refusing him penetration of her body. She feared that penetration would make her feel helpless. It was as if, by controlling his sexuality, she could control her own.

As our agreed termination date approached, Mrs C wept bitterly and dreamt that she was pregnant but could not keep her baby. She was afraid that the new baby part of herself that had grown in the course of analysis would have to be aborted by our separation. In working through the termination phase of her analysis she recognized that her pregnancies had not been in order to bear a live child, but in order concretely to assert her bodily separateness from her mother; the foetus inside her was concretely the hated mother controlling her body, whom she expelled in fantasy through the abortions. She confessed that she had enjoyed having her body to herself after each abortion, but that at another level she also knew she loved her husband and wanted his child.

Some months after she left England Mrs C wrote that she and her husband had resumed their sexual relationship, and she was thinking of starting a pregnancy. It was as if, having concretely left the bad mother of her internal world and the good mother she had found in her analyst, who encouraged her to separate and grow, she could now anticipate a new separate physical and emotional adult status.

Conclusion

Women who miscarry or consciously abort a foetus may have unconscious difficulties in identifying with a generous representation of their own mother and her capacity to mother, for the nutrient mother may be seen as a two-faced figure – as a powerful, generous, nourishing, life-giving object, or as her fantasied opposite, the witch-like murderous mother who will bring retaliation upon her daughter. Difficulty in integrating these two polarized aspects of the mother and her mothering into that of a good-enough mother may lead to a negatively ambivalent relationship between mother and daughter, to difficulties in emotional separation and identification with the murderous mother and infanticide rather than towards identification with the positive nurturing mother who gives life to her child. Fathers of these women may often have been dead, absent or emotionally detached, unable to influence the difficult relationship between these mothers and daughters.

These women may have unconsciously somatized their childhood emotional difficulties by using their bodies to avoid conscious affects and fantasies which have felt overwhelming to the young child's ego. For some women, therefore, the small girl's wish to bear a child in identification with the fertile mother may be difficult to fulfil, since her early sexual wishes and fantasies are invested in a forbidden object, her mother's sexual partner. In the child's psychic reality the oedipal wishes have become so traumatic and guilt-laden that they remain unconscious, unacknowledged and unresolved in adult life. They are therefore unavailable in adult heterosexual relationships, although the pervasive ill-defined sense of guilt may lead to an unconscious need for punishment, such as masochistic submission to a sadistic partner, or to self-punishment by miscarrying a longed-for pregnancy. The pregnant woman's normal ambivalence towards the foetus and whom it represents may be reinforced by a small girl's unacknowledged and unresolved guilt-laden wishes towards a forbidden sexual object, her mother's sexual partner. Spontaneous abortion, miscarriage, which denies life to the foetus, may provide a psychosomatic solution to this psychic conflict. If the patient is in analysis during pregnancy, analysis of her conflicts may in some cases lead to a successful pregnancy and the birth of a baby.

Note

1. It should be noted that one first pregnancy in four ends in miscarriage.

EMOTIONAL ASPECTS OF INFERTILITY AND ITS REMEDIES*

I n the course of my professional life – first as a
physician working in a London hospital where
women patients only were treated, and later as a
psychoanalyst treating both men and women – my infertile patients have made me aware of the deep emotional
suffering they experience. In the past childless couples
had two choices: either gradual conscious acceptance of
their childless state – although in my clinical experience
such an acceptance is never final – or alternatively
adoption of someone else's child. Readily available abortion drastically reduced the numbers of such children, and
it was with great relief that patients have turned to use
the enormous strides in the treatment of infertility that
have gradually become available to them over the last ten
years. These methods have brought both hope and disap-

---

* Published in *International Journal of Psycho-Analysis* (1990) 71: 561–7.

pointment to many couples, since the success rate is comparatively low.[1]

However successful these procedures may be, the couple that has resorted to artificial reproduction has had to come to terms with their failure as a couple to conceive and create life as their parents did. They must also mourn the loss of their lifelong wish and expectation that normal heterosexual activity in physically mature human beings would lead to conception and the birth of a baby, as it had done in the generation before them. Since infertility is a failure that the couple cannot deny, shame and guilt are inevitably part of their emotional predicament – shame that they cannot conceive, as so many of their friends do, and guilt that they cannot give grandchildren to their parents and in this way continue the generations of the family and their blood relationships.

My clinical experience leads me to believe that women are particularly affected by the deprivation of infertility. We know from child observation that for both sexes identification with the primary object, the powerful pre-oedipal mother, is vividly displayed throughout childhood in play and fantasy (Kestenberg, 1974, p. 156). Gender identity is established in early childhood and reinforced by parental attitudes into a core gender identity (Stoller, 1968). Sexual identity is largely resolved by adolescence. In puberty physical maturation makes it in theory possible for the first time for both sexes to fulfil their childhood wishes and fantasies. A boy may impregnate a girl, and a girl may fill her internal body space with a living and growing foetus. The complicated physiological and psychological influences of early childhood contribute to the foundation and development of the individual child, and to the establishment of his or her body image and self-representation; this must change from that of a child to that of a physically mature human being with mature genitalia capable of reproduction. This implies that, for both men and women, confidence in and awareness of their capacity to reproduce is part of their self-image. For women alone there is an additional maturational task, for although a woman's mature body concretely resembles her mother's, she is faced with the dual and conflicting tasks of identifying with her mother's female capacities whilst at the same time emotionally separating from her and taking over responsibility for her own sexuality and her own body. Pregnancy, the final stage of identification with her own mother, rooted in a bodily identification with her, contributes to the fulfil-ment of a girl child's ego-ideal, which contains her own maternal self in identification with her fertile mother. Thus we may see that for the small girl trust in her future capacity to bear a child as her mother did is critical in the confident development of her sense of femininity, sexual identity and self-esteem. These can come to frui-tion only when her body achieves physical maturity. Pregnancy fantasies and wishes may thus be seen as a normal part of the small girl's future identity, a goal to be achieved in her adult life (Pines, 1982).

Today many women, wanting to establish themselves in a career, choose to postpone pregnancy and childbirth until later, while still continuing to have faith in their reproductive capacities. Faced with the painful reality that they cannot conceive, women feel devastated, especially if physiological time is running out. Lack of control over the reproductive capacities of one's own body is an enormous personal crisis – a powerful blow to the individual's narcissism, a diminution of pride in the mature bodily self-representation, the relationship to the self, and to the sexual relationship which may seem to become mechanical, especially if fertility techniques place constraints on its spontaneity. It is not only the techniques

136

themselves, but also the expert doctors who administer them – giving or refusing permission for intercourse, and thus becoming vital figures in the intimate aspects of the couple's lives – that complicate the issue. There are now always three figures in the bed, the fourth being the analyst who observes. Thus the emotional life of a couple who already feel diminished in their sense of maturity becomes even more complicated by the conscious or unconscious regressive transference to the life-giving doctor, and to the analyst, as if they were the powerful parents of the past.

Working with infertile women has made me aware of the intensity with which many women strive to achieve fulfilment of the childhood wish to conceive and bear a child within their body, and thus attain their ego-ideal of a maternal self. In my view the crisis of infertility highlights fixation to an earlier phase of development. A young woman's experience of her own mother and of her capacity to mother, and the way her mother has dealt with her own femininity, is of prime importance in establishing her own mature female identity. Winnicott (1975) emphasized the important role of the maturational environment provided by the mother or her substitute in the primitive stages of ego development. If the baby's needs are not adequately met, then feelings of rage, frustration and hate for the mother will lead to an impoverished and empty internal world, and to a basic mistrust in the good experiences of life. Prolonged deprivation at this stage in which the child feels unsatisfied and unsatisfactory may lead to a low sense of self-esteem and a difficulty in giving and receiving love and concern later in life. As I have written in other papers, if the first experience with the pre-oedipal mother has not enabled the little girl to internalize a mutual feeling of bodily satisfaction between her mother and herself, then only with difficulty can she, make up in later stages of life for her basic loss of a primary stable sense of well-being in her body, and with the body image.

Most of the infertile women I have seen have had a difficult, conflicted and frustrating relationship with their own mothers. Many of them are high achievers in their own right, and consciously or unconsciously despise their mothers. Yet most of these same mothers have conceived and borne children easily and naturally, as their infertile daughters have not. My clinical experience with these infertile patients leads me to believe that they sustain a deep narcissistic wound and regress to a basic body image and state of mind in which they feel unsatisfied by their sexual partners and unsatisfactory to them, as they had once felt to their mothers. Unconsciously they appear to be fixated to an earlier stage of their feminine development in which they feel they have not yet been given permission by their mothers to bear their own babies. Unconsciously, despair and envy of their fertile mothers pushes them into repeated desperate attempts at fertilization despite their previous failures. Other areas of these infertile women's lives may be impoverished by the intensity of their longing to be pregnant, since the menstrual cycle and its vicissitudes become the focus of their attention. Acceptance of their inability to conceive, which would enable them to mourn their hopes and resume life, appears to be an impossible task, until the physiological changes of the menopause inevitably bring such hopes to an end.

The new infertility techniques may successfully help other women to become pregnant. However, the normal interaction between fantasy and reality that is stimulated by the adult wish for a baby (Pines, 1972) is complicated both before conception and during pregnancy by these new techniques and the transference to the donors of sperm, and to the doctors.

The first case I have chosen to illustrate my theme is of a young immature woman whose husband was sterile, so that attempted fertilization was by means of an anonymous donor. These attempts failed, and she never conceived.

The second case, which I shall describe and discuss in more detail, is of an older and more mature woman whose husband's low sperm count was improved by the new techniques, as was her own fertility. Conception was not complicated by the anonymity of the father, but the emotional aspects of pregnancy were complicated at each stage by the fertility techniques and the transference to the obstetrician.

Clinical Example 1

Mrs A had first consulted me as a seventeen-year-old adolescent. She had been depressed and sad since her mother died, leaving her nineteen-year-old sister and herself to struggle with life. Her parents had separated when Mrs A was five years old. Her mother, with her two children, moved back to poor surroundings in London, where her family lived. Mrs A's father was a weak and unsuccessful man, but she remembered his fondness for her. She had been his favourite child, and he turned to her whenever her mother made him unhappy. She felt so guilty about her fantasied childish oedipal triumph over her mother that she would not see him when he tried to contact her after the divorce.

Mrs A was a bright little girl; she did well at school and eventually went to university. Her academic success, as well as the sustained support and love that the sisters gave each other, became her main source of comfort and self-esteem. Mrs A returned to see me for one consultation some years later, full of doubt about marrying her fiancé in some weeks' time. She had been attracted to him for narcissistic reasons. He came from an intellectual milieu, one that Mrs A had always longed to belong to, and most of all he had a refined, intelligent mother whom Mrs A loved and admired, and who in return appreciated Mrs A's intelligence and achievements. Mrs A had always been ashamed of her uneducated and poor family. She had precipitately decided to marry this man when her sister unexpectedly married a foreigner and went abroad. However, just before marriage Mrs A could no longer deny her fiancé's numerous emotional difficulties, notably his lack of self-confidence and lack of success in his working life despite his excellent academic credentials, which Mrs A had envied. This had led her to consult me.

Nevertheless she married him despite her doubts, and returned to see me again some years later. This time she was extremely upset that she had not become pregnant and given birth to a baby who would love her and whom she could love, since she was aware of the lack of love in her marriage and in her life, although there was companionship and friendship. She cried bitterly about her husband's immaturity and his sterility, which had just been diagnosed. It deprived her of a further step in feminine maturation which she had longed for since she was a little girl. She said, 'Even when we make love we are like children, since we can't make a child.' Unconsciously, pregnancy would have proved her physical maturity and her husband's. Nevertheless, in the eyes of the external world Mrs A and her husband were mature, well-educated people holding down responsible jobs. Mr A's self-esteem suffered grievously from his sterility. He became even less self-assured, and felt impotent both in his work and with his wife. However, he willingly accepted his wife's determination to become pregnant and have a baby of her own. In the face of her natural anxiety over whose child she would be carrying, they consciously planned this procedure. He accompanied her every time to the consultant who artificially inseminated her, and waited for her to emerge. At night he attempted to make love to her, as if in fantasy he was the man who impregnated her, but as she showed little response he became more depressed and impotent as time went on.

To my surprise, despite this sad state of affairs, Mrs A remained cheerful and confident. Eventually she told me that she had seduced her gynaecologist. Not only did he inseminate her with donor sperm, but they made love afterwards. In this way Mrs A humanized the scientific procedure and avoided guilt-laden fantasies about who the anonymous donor might be. Consciously, the father of her future child was to be her gynaecologist. I was made to feel as if I were the child observing the parents in the bedroom. The gynaecologist always said, 'But what does your analyst think?' as if he too was aware of the situation between the four of us. I found myself in an extremely difficult situation. My anger with a colleague who betrayed a patient's trust was as intense as it might have been with a father who yielded to the seduction of a flirtatious little girl. Many times I was tempted to telephone him as if I was the mother who stopped the father from abusing his child. Yet at the same time I could not betray a patient's confidence. I was rendered as impotent as Mr A.

I began to suspect and eventually interpret that the acting-out was linked with Mrs A's early flirtatiousness with her father and her unconscious anxiety about her fantasied oedipal triumph over her mother, which would have ended in the conception of the forbidden oedipal child. For in every little girl's pregnancy wish there is an impulse to 'steal' the father from the mother, as Mrs A was stealing the gynaecologist from his wife. Thus Mrs

A's natural curiosity and anxiety about the anonymous donor who would make her pregnant revived her childhood wish to have her father's child and steal it from her mother. Mrs A did not succeed in conceiving, as if unconsciously any child conceived by her would have resulted from a forbidden guilt-laden intercourse – both in the present concretely with the gynaecologist and in the past in fantasy with her father. Interpretation of her predicament both in her past and in the present in the transference enabled her to mourn the loss of both her parents and the loss of the child she had wanted. Analysis enabled her to give up the insemination which had failed to make her pregnant.

Clinical Example 2

The second patient, Mrs B, had been in analysis with me for some years. She had not used contraception for the many years of her marriage, but had never become pregnant. Much of our work together had centred upon her feelings of inadequacy, her envy of her husband and her contempt for him if he fell below the standard she set for him by idealizing her own father. Her husband was a handsome, intelligent but passive man, deeply attached to her, and he mothered her.

Mrs B's envy of him was expressed by subtle denigration of him in whatever he did. Unconsciously, she repeated her own mother's denigration of her father when she was a child. Mr B remained potent as Mrs B's father had done, but became deeply depressed and sought analytic help for himself. Our own work centred upon Mrs B's poor self-image and her lack of pleasure in her femininity and female body. She had worn an eye-patch as a child and had had to have considerable orthodontic help to correct dental deficiencies. Her pretty mother showed little sympathy for her difficulties, had forced her to have the necessary operations but had never gone with her to hospital or been with her when she woke from the anaesthetic. It was her father who had been there when she needed him. Nevertheless, Mrs B as an adult felt that she would have become phobic if she had not been so frightened of her mother. It was better to struggle with any task, despite her anxieties, than face her mother's wrath. For her mother would beat her with a belt if she was too provocative, and force her to have enemas if she defied her control by becoming constipated. In Mrs B's internal world there was an angry ungenerous mother, an idealized father and a child with a damaged and unsatisfactory body image.

Mrs B faced much psychic pain in our work together, particularly in the area of shame both about herself and about her husband. As her self-esteem improved she began to make intimate friends, to make great strides in her work and be less aggressive to her husband. She realized that she was nearing forty and that her time for conception was nearly over. Investigation showed that her husband's sperm count was low and that they would have to use the new fertility techniques, since time was short. In the pre-conceptive stage Mrs B became deeply ashamed. It was as if, despite all her achievements, which were so much greater than her mother's, she had failed to do what her mother had done naturally without any external help. All the areas of narcissistic disappointment and shame in her childhood were revived: the eye-patch and the orthodontic treatment. She regressed to her poor self-image. In her dreams nothing was going on in her own bed. The sexual activity was in the parental bed, and she could only watch. This repeated her childhood situation of having shared her parents' bedroom, having been secretly excited by hearing and smelling their sexual activity. Since her husband could not impregnate her, it was her father who remained the potent male in her mind. Thus, in intercourse she complained that her husband's penis felt too big for her vagina, as if she had regressed to feeling the little girl whose vagina was too small to contain the penis of her mother's sexual partner – her father.

This regression was repeated in the transference, where it seemed that we were not bodily separate, as she unconsciously had not felt separate from her own mother. Whose baby would her future baby be? If she was not pregnant then I must be, and I would inevitably claim the baby as mine. Anxious fantasies followed that when her analysis ended she would have to leave the baby with me. Much was worked through regarding her difficulty in being separate from her mother, and when she became pregnant and saw the first foetal scan Mrs B was relieved to have concretely seen that the baby was in her body, not in mine. The little foetus was visible and therefore real when it was only a few weeks old, and was therefore not the baby in the mind that pregnant women normally have until the baby quickens. Thus pregnancy helped her to achieve the final stage of a biological identification with her mother and reinforced a more adult sense of being separate from her. However, although she never doubted that she was pregnant with her husband's child, the fertility techniques which excluded intercourse confirmed her denigration of his potency. Her obstetrician was in fantasy the father of her child, the godlike father of her childhood. Thus one of the tasks of pregnancy – the integration of the representation of the sexual partner as father to the foetus – was interfered with. She continued to denigrate her husband, since he was not her sexual partner in their present reality, and refused in her mind to acknowledge his share in the conception of the baby. It was as if the foetus were the doll which she had always refused to share with her sister. It was also as if the fantasied hidden penis, the little man inside her – in fantasy her father's – had enabled her omnipotently to conceive her own child. She had done it all by herself, as she had done many other things in her life, and in this way she could deny the painful reality of not having been able to be in control of her own bodily functions.

Amniocentesis showed that Mrs B was carrying a healthy little boy, and the material of the next few months in analysis enabled us to work through her hatred and anger towards men. Regression in pregnancy in identification with the foetus emphasized her childhood anxieties, which had not been contained by her parents. It enabled her to appreciate her husband's mothering qualities as well as the dependable qualities of her obstetrician and her analyst, as if they had become in fantasy the powerful united devoted parents she had not had in her childhood. Mrs B felt firmly held by both of us. My task was to monitor and analyse her ambivalence towards herself, her femininity, the foetus, and all the figures in her life, and in this way enable her to achieve a more positive aspect of ambivalence. Thus we approached the second phase of normal pregnancy, in which fantasies about the foetus that begins to stir in a woman's body revive regressive fantasies about bodily contents.

Now Mrs B re-experienced her desperate need for being mothered in the course of her pregnancy, and the re-emergence of previously repressed fantasies, as in all pregnant women, enabled them to be worked through in analysis. In particular, analysis of the early mother–child relationship with her own mother enabled her to avoid identification with the conflictual introjected bad mother of her internal world, and make a different choice. She became a devoted mother once her child was born. It should be noted that the frequent scanning of the foetus, with its concrete pictures, also enabled Mrs B to avoid the normal anxieties of pregnancy regarding the foetus. For, in accordance with childhood sexual theories, a pregnant woman may fear that the foetus may be a potentially devouring destructive creature within her body, or a shameful and dirty object that the mother must expel as the little girl expelled faeces in her childhood. The concrete appearance of the foetus and its visual growth and development also enabled Mrs B to bond with her baby in pregnancy. In this way the new object relationship with the baby began much earlier than usual, since for most mothers it begins only when the baby separates from the mother's body and emerges into the object world. Paradoxically, for both Mrs B and her analyst her pregnancy seemed to have gone on far beyond the normal span, for the organization of time was disturbed by such an early bonding with the foetus.

Mrs B's second pregnancy was again aided by the new fertility techniques. This time her husband's sperm count was better, but her own ovarian supply was affected by her ageing. This was another blow to her self-esteem, but since so much of the internal world of her childhood had been worked through in analysis in her first pregnancy and she was now a happy mother in her adult state, she accepted the necessity of further medical intervention. Three eggs were extracted and fertilized, but this time it seemed that bonding with the foetus began with the finding of the egg. Mr and Mrs B were as excited as if she were actually pregnant. Two of the eggs could not be fertilized, and in her dreams Mrs B mourned them as if they were two dead babies. Finally Mrs B became pregnant again, but there was some anxiety about the possibility of an early miscarriage. The foetus was scanned very early on, and this time Mrs B found it hard to believe that it was *inside* her, since there were as yet no changes

146

in her body, as there had been in her first pregnancy. Although she bled and was advised to rest, it was not until I became angry with her that she gave in, for my anger reinforced the adult part of herself and fought the regressive aspects of pregnancy. Eventually what emerged was her terror that as she was over forty she might be carrying an abnormal child, and that until she could have an amniocentesis she could not allow herself to bond with the foetus, in case she would have to murder a person. This time, seeing the foetus was an additional burden. She was preoccupied with the concrete mechanics of her fertilization and thus avoided the emotional aspects.

As the pregnancy progressed and she became more tired and regressed, she complained that she had no memory of a passionate adult sexual encounter at conception to comfort her and remind her of her adulthood. She allowed herself to express her anger about being made to feel she was only a container for the foetus by her husband, her obstetrician and her analyst. Her primacy was threatened, since the machinery controlled her conception and her pregnancy (as did her obstetrician and her analyst). Thus quickening, an event that excites most pregnant women, was a non-event for both of us in the transference and for her husband and herself in reality, since she was still so anxious about the fate of the baby. Our attention was focused on external help and observation rather than on her own mind and body communication. She felt robbed of the experience that other women had in this way. Yet despite the concrete details of conception, of which her obstetrician always informed her, Mrs B continued to comfort herself in her fantasy life and revive her childhood sexual theories. Although she had been told accurately about the details of her treatment, in her fantasy the egg was laid next to the sperm and they fertilized each other in a cosy spot in her womb

– symbolically mother and father tucked up in their bed in the bedroom she had shared with them, and where her mother had conceived.

A dream at this time revealed some of her internal predicament and the maturational growth that had occurred. In the dream she was standing in the backyard of her childhood home. Children had been abused there, and she hated being there again. It was squalid and her parents were quarrelling, as usual. Strange plants were growing there; they looked like castrated penises. As she looked beyond the wall she saw a new development with a path leading to it. There was grass in the garden. In her associations Mrs B recognized that her present life was much better than her childhood, and that she had matured in analysis. Her obstetrician and her analyst were powerful helpful parents who unitedly held her without splitting or quarrelling as her childhood parents had done. The child she already had enabled her and her husband to become close and united parents, and the green grass represented her new-found hope that the foetus was growing well inside her womb. She was fearful that the castrated penises were the handicap that would make her want to abort a boy. The castrated penises also showed her identification with the foetus, since at the beginning of her analysis she had behaved like a castrated boy. The boy foetus represented her own handicaps, and signified that there was still time to work things through in her pregnancy. She reminded herself how much she loved her son in the present. At the end of the session she exclaimed with delight that she felt relieved, and the foetus, which had been quiet for several hours, had moved again. She hoped all would be well.

Finally, the task every woman has to accomplish in order to fulfil her childhood wish to conceive and bear a child is to integrate reality with unconscious fantasy, hopes and daydreams. The move from childlessness to parenthood, the final stage of both biological and emotional identification with her own mother, revives conflicts from the earlier stages in her development, and the young woman has to find new accommodations within both her inner world and the outer object world. The revival of unconscious oedipal and pre-oedipal conflicts and fantasies that occurs in every pregnancy may be even more complicated if in reality the sexual partner of a woman's adult life has not been able to impregnate her. A couple's failure to conceive, the concrete nature of the fertility techniques and the transference to the godlike, life-giving obstetrician impose an additional task to the integration of reality with past conscious and unconscious fantasies, hopes and daydreams. In my view, psychoanalysis provides invaluable emotional support in working through some of the complicated issues that must be faced in this type of pregnancy.

The external despair which drives infertile women to repeated attempts at fertilization mirrors their internal despair at not being able to control their bodies. Frequently they strive in analysis to regain an omnipotent stance by means of knowing more about their bodies and thus hoping to regain control of them. Repeated unsuccessful attempts at fertilization may become a way of avoiding the eventual mourning of the childhood wishes and adult hope for the birth of a child. These couples are preoccupied with monthly success or failure in conception, at the cost of much of their adult investment in life.

It may become the analyst's task to enable these women to give up hope and to come to terms with the harsh reality that they cannot conceive. Although in my experience sadness remains, and hope is never relinquished until the menopause, the patient can, if she is helped to mourn, recover her self-esteem in other areas of her life and find satisfaction elsewhere.

Note

1. The new procedures to help a woman to become pregnant are as follows: AIH, artificial insemination by the husband's sperm if he is impotent or his sperm count is too low; AID with donor sperm, if the sexual partner is sterile or one is not available; *in vitro* fertilization, in which the woman's eggs are surgically removed, fertilized *in vitro* and then returned to her womb, where, it is hoped, pregnancy will continue and culminate in the birth of a healthy baby. A new development named 'the gift' enables the egg to be mixed with the sperm and returned to the fallopian tube to be fertilized rather than being held *in vitro*.

THE MENOPAUSE

During the past few years a higher proportion of women in their fifties and sixties have come into my practice than I have seen before. Very little has been written about the later stages of a woman's life, and I am grateful to my patients who – approaching, reaching and passing through the menopause – have shared their pleasure and their pain with me. They have taught me to empathize with and respect each individual's struggle to come to terms with this later stage of the life cycle, with the inevitable loss of past youth and fertility, and with the anticipation of future loss of important figures in their lives.

Since medical knowledge and care have improved the quality of the last third of a woman's life, the menopause may mark the start of a new and vigorous phase, largely unknown to the previous generation; life expectancy for a woman is now thirty years longer than it was fifty years ago. Despite this, the same emotional problems of separation and losses must be faced – the loss of children leaving home, the future loss of ageing parents who may need to be cared for, and the inevitable future loss of one's own life or that of a spouse. Since life is now finite rather than infinite, as it seemed to be in the earlier phases of the life cycle, the knowledge that all human relationships must end may add zest to the post-menopausal years. Life is divided into two parts: the ascent to the peak of the mid-life crisis and the decline after this mid-point towards old age and death. For a woman the tasks of earlier adult life – child-bearing and child-rearing – are over, and she must now decide how she wants her own unaccustomed space to be filled by being what she wants to be for herself rather than fulfilling the needs of others.

A sense of loss is unavoidably experienced by both sexes, and mourning for childhood, youth and young adulthood paves the way to a new phase of life. For women in particular the bodily signs and symptoms of ageing – flushing, drying of the skin and mucous membranes, which may cause vaginal dryness and dyspareunia, thus complicating sexuality – are difficult to bear. Thus, ageing is associated with the finality of the ending of reproduction. Some women who continue to menstruate after they know they have become infertile welcome their periods as a sign that they are still young and desirable. The use of hormone replacement therapy has enabled women to retain a more youthful appearance, since their skin and general sense of well-being sometimes respond dramatically to it. The danger of osteoporosis, where fragile bone structure may lead to broken bones and handicap, is averted. Many of my older patients enjoy life to the full, and are active, valuable members of their families and communities.

Despite the possible postponement of visible ageing,

however, the final cessation of menstruation unavoidably marks the end of a woman's child-bearing years. A fertile, creative phase that began in puberty is now over. Some women who have not borne children or consciously wanted them until it was too late may still deeply mourn the ending of the possibility of being pregnant as their mothers had been. The wish to be pregnant must be differentiated from the wish to have a child. For a woman whose supreme pleasure has been the conception, birth and mothering of children, coming to terms with this loss may be one of the most difficult tasks in her life. Never again can a foetus be contained in her womb, and never again can a child be born to fill so much of the mother's life. Helene Deutsch (1944) describes this time as an experience of partial death – that is, the death of a woman's reproductive functions – but writing nearly fifty years later, I am more impressed by the post-menopausal zest that many women experience once they have passed through the unsettling transitional phase.

My clinical experience leads me to believe that though a woman may have made a conscious decision to have no more children some time ago, there is always the possibility of a new baby in her mind until the gradual onset of the menopause and its unavoidable physical signs destroy her hopeful fantasy and sense of eternal youth. A patient told me that when she looked in the mirror she felt that she could not look like her reflection, since she did not feel like that. Thus there may be a discrepancy between the subjective youthful body image and the objective older image. Some women may conceive a child very late in life in order to continue their youth and postpone the ending of fertility.

My clinical experience has also led to my understanding that the wish for a child is not universal, and that for many women who have not enjoyed their sexuality,

153

childbirth or child-rearing, the menopause may be a relief, allowing them to develop other areas of creativity and other interests and occupations to fill their lives. Sexuality may be much freer and more pleasurable if there is no longer a possibility of pregnancy. For these women, therefore, the menopause may provide a new stimulus towards further maturational development and psychic growth. Most of the older women in my practice are professionals whose sense of self-esteem is not grounded in their youth and feminine attractiveness alone, but also in their professional skills and achievements, which grow with experience. For them post-menopausal development, the freedom of sexual life without conception and mature relationships may be rewarding, since in my view adult psychological growth continues throughout life and is bound neither to biological development nor to decline. The experience of loss and mourning for an earlier phase of development can therefore eventually be liberating. However, women whose professional lives depend upon bodily youth and attractiveness may react with deep depression and anger to the unavoidable physical signs of change (I. Hellman, 1992, personal communication).

Although the subject of the menopause has received little attention, some women analysts have written about it. Deutsch (1945) maintains that the 'climacteric is a narcissistic mortification that is difficult to overcome'. She asserts that 'a woman has a complicated emotional life that is not restricted to motherhood, thus she may succeed in actively finding a way out of the biological'. However, 'everything a woman has gained by puberty is now lost piece by piece and the psychological decline is felt as the proximity of death'. Benedek (1950) takes a more optimistic approach. In her view 'the struggle between sexual drives and the ego which begins at puberty diminishes or ends with the climactericum. This frees a woman from conflicts around sexuality and gives her spare energy, providing a new impetus for socialisation and learning'. Lax (1982) describes the menopause as a 'psychic crisis which women experience during this phase in the light of their sense of body integrity, their sense of bodily functioning, their self-image and their life tasks and ego interests'. Notman (1982) also subscribes to a more optimistic point of view, and concludes that possibilities for post-menopausal expansion do exist: 'The potential for greater autonomy, changes in relationships and the development of occupational skills and an expanded self-image may receive a major impetus after child bearing is over.' However, she also asserts that 'depression has been linked with the menopause and it constitutes an important clinical entity'.

In my experience, for women who have had children the depression may be linked to the children's adolescence, to their struggle to separate from the parents which eventually leads to their leaving home, rather than to the menopause itself. The parents have to readjust to becoming a couple on their own again – a task that may require considerable work, since problems that have been obscured by family life tend to re-emerge. The mother has also lost the lively bustle of the children and their friends that filled the home. Her life may seem lonely and empty. This may lead to brooding on the time that has passed, and to depression and sadness. Also at this time, a foetus that was aborted from the mother's body – though not from her mind – in her youth may be brought to life as the child who was never born, whom the mother must now mourn deeply, since she can no longer have children. As at every phase of the life cycle, mourning is inevitable until a new phase can open up new vistas. For women who have not had children and can now no longer hope for them, the sense of loss and emptiness may be particularly painful.

Lax, in 'The expectable depressive climacteric reaction' (1982), provides a most helpful and extensive review of the current literature on the menopause, and concludes that 'a woman can use her resources during the climacteric interval to work through the narcissistic injury and reconstitute a meaningful life for herself . . .' A successful outcome depends in large measure on the woman's adaptive capacities, her libidinal resources and her skills, as well as on the culture in which she lives. In cultures where ageing is linked with wisdom and respect, a grandmother becomes the matriarchal centre of a family.

'Change of life', as it is frequently called, is an apt term for this phase of a woman's life, in which so much must change in her view of herself, her body, her body image, and the self-esteem that has in many cases been gained through other people's admiration of her youthful appearance. Thus the anxieties of the adolescent girl are revived in the anxieties of the menopausal and post-menopausal woman – once again body image and attractiveness to others become important factors in a woman's view of herself.

I have chosen four clinical examples to illustrate my theme. The first is of a woman who had to make a choice between reverting to the unhappy patterns of her life as a pre-pubertal child and moving on to a new kind of creativity.

Mrs A, who had divorced her husband much earlier in her life, was aware of her approaching menopause. Her periods were becoming irregular, and she knew they would soon stop. She had a good professional job, and was on warm, friendly terms with her two adult children. Several affairs with men had ended, but since she feared repeating an unhappy marriage, life on her own was not unsatisfying. She knew she was still attractive and had hopes of meeting a man she would be happy with.

In her dream Mrs A found herself standing at a cross-roads. She remembered that there had been a beautiful flower bed, but it was now concreted over. One road led up a hill towards the house where she had been an unhappy only child. She did not know the other road, but it was there for her to take. In her associations to her dream Mrs A regretted that her child-bearing years were now at an end – the beautiful flower bed was now concreted over – but she realized that she no longer had to regress to the unhappy pre-pubertal child she once was – she was clear that she now had an adult self to sustain her. Her child-bearing years had been the happiest of her life. She knew that she was attractive and intelligent, with a profession and a role in the world, and that now she had a choice which the unhappy child had not had. Many other forms of creativity lay ahead on the unknown road of adult life.

My second example concerns a patient for whom the menopause was a particularly severe personal crisis because it brought to the surface lifelong problems and confusions she had had about the death of her father when she was a very small child. Mrs B came to London from Scotland when she was seventeen years old. She was a lively, pretty girl who spoke with an attractive Scottish burr, which persists until this day. Her warm, open-hearted ways soon won her friends, and within two years she met and married her present husband. He was an older, stronger man who, she felt, would protect her and care for her as her father might have done had he lived.

Mrs B's father had been killed in the War when she was three. The only visual memory she had of him was of his bright-blue eyes looking tenderly into hers, and she also remembered feeling strongly held and protected when he carried her on his broad shoulders towards the woods which surrounded her village. At first she easily accepted her mother's story that he had gone into the woods and not returned. When her mother later told her the truth about his death, Mrs B accepted it without much reaction, since she was unable to mourn a father she had hardly known. Marriage and the change of identity from a single woman to a married one appeared to present little difficulty to her. In fact she now lived in a double reality, for – as with many traumatized people – part of her continued to live as the little girl she had been when her father was killed, as if time had stood still then. Another part of her, however, had continued to grow and mature into adult life. Thus she lived in the double reality of the present and the past. This confusion was accentuated by Mrs B's mother being brought into the marriage, since Mrs B could not separate from her. Her husband accepted the situation and encouraged both women's dependence on him.

In Mrs B's mind, her husband was a replacement for the strong father she had barely known. In fantasy her husband was both her mother's sexual partner – i.e. her father – and her own lover. Thus unconsciously it was as if her sexual pleasure was a forbidden triumph over her mother, and her three children were her father's children. This fantasy was further encouraged by her mother sharing the care of the children with her, as if they were both the mothers of the children. So in fantasy her children were also her siblings. As Mrs B's children entered adolescence she went through similar feelings and began to find her husband's attitude controlling and difficult, as if she too was her husband's adolescent daughter. She was passing through an adolescent phase that she had not experienced in her own development. She became confused and unhappy, resented her mother's presence in the house, and gave up her sexual life with her husband. Both husband and wife became depressed, and Mrs B was referred to me for therapy. As we worked through the confusion that existed in her mind between her children and herself and her husband and her father, Mrs B gradually came to terms with her real father's death and the loss of the fantasy of him that had been displaced on to her husband. She was able to give up the double reality in which she had been living, and to see herself as wife and mother.

A dream that Mrs B had towards the end of her analysis was particularly important in resolving this confusion. In the dream she was still menstruating in her late forties, and she had been carrying a white bag around with her for nearly a month. In the bag was a baby with a slightly wrinkled skin. She went to the doctor and opened the bag. The baby's skin looked tanned, as Mrs B's always did; and she said to the doctor, 'Isn't it a lovely baby?' The doctor said, 'Yes, but it's dead.' My patient was horrified and said, 'But it's moving.' The doctor again answered, 'But it's dead.' My patient woke up in deep distress. As Mrs B thought about the dream, she told me that she had always longed for another child, but her husband had become sterile after an illness. The wish for that last child therefore had to be consciously given up and mourned. This dream revealed that the longing for another child had continued to exist in her unconscious mind as long as she was menstruating, and now she knew that she could conceive no more babies. Gynaecological investigations confirmed that she could no longer conceive – a fact that her body had communicated to her in the dream. Mrs B wept bitterly as she mourned the ending of the reproductive period of her life and recognized the signs of ageing in herself: the baby with the wrinkled skin. The dream had shown that in part of her mind Mrs B still could not separate from her own mother, was still the baby in her mother's womb; hence in the dream her own mother was still young and not of an age to die.

Mrs B consoled herself with the thought that her daughter would one day have children, and that she, in identification with her, would enjoy pregnancy and child-rearing again. She also consoled herself for the pain of no longer being able to be pregnant herself. In the dream she did not know if the sack was her daughter's or her own; thus in mourning the end of her child-rearing years she found that she could adapt to 'the change of life' and hope to continue emotional mothering and motherliness, since these are not affected by physical bodily changes.

Mrs C was referred to me in a state of deep shock and distress. She was an attractive, intelligent woman of forty-seven, but her world had fallen apart when, after twenty-five years of marriage, her husband had told her that he had had a mistress in another part of the country for some years, and now had a five-year-old child by her. Mrs C had thought that their marriage was a happy and con-tented one, and had never suspected anything else. She herself had been faithful to her husband and had enjoyed their family life. They had met as students, married as soon as they could afford it, and in the course of time had had three daughters and two sons. As her husband's business had prospered, Mrs C had gradually given up her job as an architect and devoted herself to her family and their busy social life. Looking back, she realized that she had gradually become less interested in sex, since she enjoyed so much else about their life together.

Mrs C had been satisfied with her large family, had not wanted more children, and the ending of her child-bearing years was not a problem to her. It appeared, however, that this was not so in her husband's case. He had been an only child, and his own children were a source of great delight and pleasure; he had always shared the care of them with his wife, so her menopause became a crisis for him. Mr C had also struggled with his growing sexual attraction to his pretty young daughters as his sexual attraction to his post-menopausal wife waned. His daughters were embarrassed by his attentions, and his exaggerated cuddling and kissing made them uneasy. Mr C was totally unaware of his envy of younger men, his sons and his daughters' boyfriends. Not surprisingly – feeling guilty about his sexual need for a younger woman who wanted him and could still bear children – he displaced his desires from his daughters to one of their young friends. He felt that his youth was renewed with his young partner, who could still bear children. Both of them wanted and enjoyed their child, and eventually Mr C's love for this child and his guilt about his double life pushed him to confess everything to his wife.

Mrs C was shattered by this blow. It was as if an abyss had opened and cracked what had seemed to be the solid foundation of her life. However, she was sustained by the solidarity and loyal support of her children, who returned the loyal mothering she had given them by mothering her now that she needed it. Throughout her childhood her own mother had loved her deeply and been proud of her clever daughter, so she had a healthy sense of her own worth despite the crushing blow her husband had dealt her. Nevertheless, she felt as if part of her had been destroyed by her husband's betrayal. She lay listlessly in bed and came to her sessions with great difficulty, often brought by one of her children.

Gradually Mrs C came to life as she allowed herself to express her outrage and wish for revenge on her husband, yet at the same time her maternal self felt pity for his illegitimate child. As she worked through her painful feelings, she felt renewed strength. She resumed her old profession, and her success there reinforced her sense of self-esteem. Gradually she realized that she could not mend her marriage, since she sensed that she would always feel unsafe with her husband. She urged him to divorce her to make his child legitimate, and her children supported her decision.

Some years after her therapy had finished, Mrs C asked to see me again. She told me that her professional life was now very successful and that she had met a male colleague, a widower, who had fallen passionately in love with her and, since he had no children of his own, welcomed her children into his life. They were about to be married. She told me that since we had shared so much sorrow, she wanted to share her joy with me. I, who had seen her so disintegrated, was delighted by her recovery and renewed flowering. Mr C, on the contrary, left his second wife as she aged, and has since taken up with another young woman. He deeply regretted the loss of his first wife and had tried to return to her, but it was too late.

Mrs D had experienced each phase of a woman's life cycle when it was almost too late for her. She had begun her periods when she was eighteen and lived at home until her late thirties, when she managed to separate from her parents and marry. Analysis of Mrs D's internal world revealed that she felt more like a man than a woman, and identified more with her father than with her mother.

Each fresh phase of her feminine bodily identity had been difficult to accept, since each time the masculine/feminine conflict was revived. The acceptance of femininity entailed giving up her masculine identification with her father. Thus just as her first period was long delayed, so was the conscious knowledge of her wish to have a child suppressed.

She still had regular periods, which she was pleased about, since they made her feel young and fertile. What she did not know consciously was that she was no longer ovulating regularly, and her fertile time was coming to an end. However, a dream suggested that unconsciously she was in touch with her bodily hormonal change. In the dream Mrs D was trying on a jacket in which the white lining was on the outside. She said to herself, 'Run home quickly and clear things out before the police come.' Unconsciously she had noticed that her periods were shorter and the flow was less heavy; hence the lining – the uterus lining – was paler than it had been in her youth. She recognized that she was now desperate to have a baby, even to the point of wanting to steal her friend's fertility, or her mother's, or mine in the transference, since in her fantasy I was a very fertile woman with many children. Her husband had been ambivalent about her having a baby, since he was much older, but at that moment he seemed to be in a positive mood and she felt she must steal a baby from him immediately.

In due course Mrs D became pregnant, but she was unable to keep the pregnancy and miscarried. She was advised to wait some months before trying again – since time was short, this was a period of deep frustration. She dreamt that her gynaecologist diagnosed her as suffering from carcinoma of the cervix. In the dream she was not afraid of her cancer, a malignant disease which threatened her life, but angrily accepted that she could not try for babies that month. She felt dead in herself – an identification with the dead foetus – and came to life only after intercourse, when her hope was renewed that this time she would be pregnant with a baby that would live. Intercourse confirmed her female sexual identity, and pregnancy, she felt, would confirm her youth and fertility. She was afraid of old age and becoming like her own mother, who was frail and deteriorating. Not getting pregnant, however much she tried, was a terrible blow, since not being in control of her own body made her feel that she was a helpless child again. In her dreams she was always pregnant with a little girl – that is, with her baby-self, to whom she was a mother as she felt her own mother had not been to her. Each time in the dreams the pregnancy ended in miscarriage, as if this was the trauma she could not overcome – namely, her failure to become a better mother than her own mother had been to her. She experienced deep inconsolable pain that she would not have a child to look after her in her old age as she now looked after her own mother.

As time went on and her attempts to become pregnant were unsuccessful, Mrs D was frightened by her conscious wish to steal a baby from its pram. She watched her husband's sisters and her friends with jealous eyes, until in a dream she heard her youngest sister-in-law comforting a crying baby. Thus Mrs D unconsciously knew that her sister-in-law was pregnant before she was told. Mrs D was deeply distressed after the pregnancy was revealed to the family. She was enraged with all the women in her family, and with me in the transference, because we had all achieved what she could not do. She wept bitterly about her shame, and her feelings of despair and emptiness. How would she ever be able to fill this enormous gap in her life? She was overwhelmed with feelings of frustration, envy and rage when any new baby was born, and could visit mother and baby only after a tremendous effort of self-control. At a family reunion the women talked about the abortions they had had, and Mrs D said to herself sorrowfully, 'I am a barren woman.'

Dreams of loneliness confirmed her deep sadness. In many of them Mrs D was travelling in boats, trains or aeroplanes on long journeys, and always alone. She spoke mournfully about her parents ageing and there being no children to travel with her in life as she had travelled with her parents. She was in constant pain about her childlessness, and nothing would console her. In other dreams the ending of her child-bearing years was tragic. In one dream she was lying on a marble slab as if she was in a coffin, as if she had to accept the partial death of part of herself, since her child-rearing years were over. In another she had been to the hairdresser to cut her long hair off, since the style was too youthful for her now. In the dream she took a wig off, and her long hair was still there. We understood that middle age felt like a masquerade to her. Beneath the mask of her ageing face and body there still lay the young woman of her earlier body image. She longed to return to her youth and regain her chance to have a baby, since she now felt that she was an empty shell of a woman. In further dreams, whenever her ambitions at work could not be realized, she dreamt of bleeding from a miscarriage or an abortion. It was as if she felt her femininity had been excised.

Once, in a conscious fantasy during a session, she became very frightened that I was standing over her with a knife and surgically removing something from her chest. From her associations we understood that she experienced her barrenness as if I, in my consulting room, had become the sadistic mother who had removed her fertility. Mrs D's analysis was painful for both of us, since we both felt impotent in the face of irreversible physiological reality.

165

However, new possibilities of sublimation and creativity gradually appeared, and the deep pain and mourning came to an end. Acceptance of the painful reality enabled Mrs D to feel that she was still a woman despite her childlessness, and to take up new interests.

The menopause that marks the end of child-bearing years may prove a relief to women in cultures where no contraception is available and a child is born yearly, whether the mother desires it or not. In our culture, if pregnancy and childbirth have been a difficult phase in a woman's life, often accompanied by postnatal depression, the ending of the child-bearing years may bring relief and serenity. Sexuality may be more rewarding for both partners if there is no longer the danger of an unwanted pregnancy.

A woman who has had problems with her unresolved sexual identity, however, may suddenly experience a desperate wish to become pregnant. Unconsciously, she may wish to show her mother that she can nurture her child more successfully than her mother did. Frustration of this overwhelming wish may lead to deep pain and depression, which may never be totally resolved. Even a woman who has borne a child and enjoyed it may none the less need to mourn the ending of a creative phase of the life cycle which began at puberty and ended with the menopause. Such mourning, if it is worked through and completed, may lead to fresh areas of creativity.

OLD AGE

The ancient Greeks believed that 'those whom the gods love die young'. Theirs was an age when youth and physical beauty were highly valued, and death was in theory preferable to the gradual physical decline of ageing which those of us who survive have to observe in ourselves and others, and come to terms with. For most of us, survival – and life itself – are to be cherished and enjoyed for as long as possible. For a woman, much depends upon her previous experiences during the past phases of the life cycle, and whether her memories are pleasurable or unpleasurable. For now we must all face a new and unaccustomed phase of life – that of old age and death, in which the ending of our lives and the lives of those we love are inescapable facts. Nevertheless, these final years of a woman's life may also be times of further emotional growth and the reworking of past conflicts. Many older patients seek therapy for lifelong emotional problems in order to understand themselves and others better, hoping for a wiser and more serene way of life. Thus old age may be a time for continued growth and evolution rather than just a period of loss and diminished capabilities.

In old age, as in adolescence, the body resumes its important role in a woman's life. Her own good health – hitherto taken for granted – becomes more central. She is no longer preoccupied with the welfare of her children, who have now left home. Unconscious conflicts and thoughts which are unthinkable may force the body to act out as it has in the past. The small fluctuations of physical well-being to which we are all subject may seem in fantasy to be precursors of fatal diseases. Although most of the time the activity of life pushes away the idea of death, as we grow older it becomes more difficult to deny. The shadow of death now walks with us all, as in the medieval paintings of the 'danse macabre', and is present at all the celebrations of life. Even in the midst of a busy life, ageing and death cast their shadow – at the end of a holiday there can no longer be a certainty that next year we will all meet again as we have always done. Time is no longer to be taken for granted but to be cherished. Physical ageing thus undermines omnipotence.

Older patients in analysis may rapidly develop an erotic transference to the analyst, as if their outwardly aged appearance were a theatrical mask behind which lies a live and pulsating mind and body which could not be used at an appropriate time earlier in life. It is as if the urgency of time passing relieves patients of the fear of humiliation and shame that inhibited them from showing their feelings at an earlier moment, and now is the only chance to fill the gaps. There may be a reawakening of oedipal conflicts, and bisexual solutions may be more easily permitted if the stern superego and defences of earlier phases of life are weakened and the imminence of death is denied by life, interests and sexuality. Touching and being touched remains very important in old age. The foreplay of sexuality revives the earliest pleasures of the mother–infant relationship, which for many was deeply satisfying; as does the touch of a compassionate doctor or nurse, which the patient may seek for comfort in frequent hypochondriacal medical consultations. To be touched gently is a confirmation of existence, love and being cared for, and it remains very important, as it was in the beginning.

During the course of her analysis, an older woman patient, Mrs L, who had been beautiful in her youth and still remained beautiful in the later years of her life, became aware of sexual feelings that she had not allowed herself to experience earlier in life. She had married and had children, and had apparently achieved a mature identity as a woman. Yet her sexuality was only a bodily response to her husband's body; her emotions and deeper feelings were frozen and unavailable to her. After working through some of this material, Mrs L dreamt that she saw her house full of the children she had borne and heard her husband's deep voice occupying the space. Yet in another part of the house she herself lay weeping deeply and inconsolably on the analytic couch. The noise of her husband and the children was silenced as they listened. She felt that I had listened carefully, and she could now confront aspects of herself that she had never revealed before, even to herself. She could now allow that deprived part of herself to be heard, despite the outward show of husband and children. Old age was approaching, and she was mourning the loss of her youthful passionate self that had been split off in adolescence, so that the deeper aspects of sexuality had not been integrated into her adult life and now never could be.

Despite their accurate perception of the physical changes of ageing, women seem to retain a more obvious bodily narcissism than do men. An older woman is often more meticulous about her physical appearance; her hair and face are carefully groomed, as though the inescapable effects of physical ageing did not limit a woman's erotic fantasies and desires. At the same time her desirability as a sexual woman needs to be reaffirmed by external admiration, whether by a man or another woman. A woman's subjective body image is of great importance, and the mirror is a narcissistic woman's greatest enemy.

Mrs M, an older woman who had been attractive in her youth, spoke with fury of her wrinkled face and sagging breasts. She told me that when she saw herself reflected in a shop window she felt that her body had been invaded by an unknown older woman who was a stranger. Despite her rage, she felt impotent and could not repel her. Looking like her old mother gave her no comfort in old age, since that same narcissistic mother had given her daughter no comfort when she needed it in her childhood. This anger was projected on to men of her own age who, she claimed, hated her, although younger men were still attracted to her. Mrs M certainly did not consciously know about the oedipal legends and their influence on psychic life, yet she knew instinctively, as do all attractive older women, that the young Oedipus-son could evoke in his Jocasta-mother a sexual response which could be acted out or repressed.

*

An older woman's body image frequently reminds her of the older image of her mother. This was strikingly illustrated in a documentary film in which survivors of the Gulag talked about their experiences after release. One old woman described her preparations for her deportation to Siberia, where her husband had been taken. Her own mother had been closely involved in her life, so she entrusted her children to her before she was imprisoned and exiled. She and her fellow women prisoners became resigned to their terrible fate, and gave up hope. Even memories of better times no longer relieved their apathy and depression. One day they were transported to another camp; on the station there was a mirror, the first they had looked into for twenty years. This woman crowded round with her fellow prisoners, but could not find her own image until suddenly she found her mother's; then she recognized it as herself and knew she was old. Yet this was a comfort, for her face was now a link with a happier past and with her good mother who had loved her and her children. She knew that her mother must be dead by now, but the memory of better times that she had recovered gave her more strength in her terrible life.

Old age is a time in all our lives when we must be prepared for loss – both of aspects of ourselves and of companions who have accompanied us through our life's journey. Even if we are fortunate enough to be in robust health, we must accept a diminution of our own strength; we may tire more easily than we did, both physically and mentally. We must accept our declining powers of independent survival, and our progressive dependence on others. All this may be bearable, but the loss of a spouse and the gradual loss of friends may lead to a sense of loneliness which is difficult to bear. With whom can one share new thoughts, laugh with over old memories? Fortunately for some women, children, grandchildren and younger friends help to fill the gap. As at all stages of life, much depends on a person's previous history, on what has led to happiness and fulfilment, or to unhappiness and resentment. We are also influenced by the extent to which we are able to be sad and relinquish what is past in order to find fresh sources of contentment.

We all know old women who seem to have preserved the wide-eyed wonder of a child, a delight in new knowledge and experience as well as memories of past happy life events in childhood, adolescence and maturity. These women are frequently highly valued members of their family who have found new ways of benevolent parenting once their own children have grown up and gone away. The natural envy of youth and vigour which exists in most older people may be outweighed by the pleasures of grandparenthood, which repeat the earlier pleasures of parenthood and yet have an added dimension in old age – that of continuing life and the family beyond one's own lifespan. Fortunate grandparents and grandchildren have a special relationship, and the needs of both generations may be generously met. Grandparents may have the virtues of the wise elders who retain links with previous generations of ancestors, remember and maintain the family past and present. Grandparents may also see comforting aspects of themselves in their grandchildren, who may identify with them – aspects which will live on after them. So grandparenthood may be a valuable reinforcement to a core sense of one's personal identity. The son or daughter of the next generation may be an unexpected delight if they fill the space in the mind left by the son or daughter who was not born in the previous generation. Retirement from a busy professional life may be compensated for by increased leisure and space for grandchildren, and renewed intimate relationships with family and friends.

Mrs N, a stylish eighty-year-old, talked about the import-ance to her of remaining intellectually busy as her age increasingly limited her physical strength. She had had a traumatic early history in that at the age of ten she was abruptly separated from her depressed mother and sent abroad for ten years by her enraged father. He had never forgiven her mother for a family tragedy that she had inadvertently caused. Mrs N's mother had been feeding her first child with plums, which she carefully de-stoned. A friend had been visiting her; she escorted her to the door and talked for a while. When she came back she found, to her horror, that the baby in the highchair had reached to the plums on the table, and choked to death on a stone.

Mrs N had frequently longed for her mother in her exile, and wept about her loss. Gradually she had over-come the pain of longing by keeping herself busy with intellectual pursuits, by learning and studying her future profession. Thus she learnt to deal with the painful losses of adult life, just as she had learnt to deal with her childhood pain at a very early age. She could use her mind to give her comfort. Mrs N's children left her country and settled abroad, although they were in fre-quent touch with her. When she was widowed she studied a new science, and eventually began to teach it. So loneliness, pain and longing were countered by additional intellectual achievements which introduced her to a fresh circle of friends, among whom was a man of her own age who courted her and helped her to feel that she was still a desirable woman. When Mrs N was alone, she fondly remembered her husband. Memories of the happy times they had spent together as adults enabled her to overcome the traumatic childhood separation from her dearly beloved mother, and becoming a mother herself had filled her life. Identifying with her successful children also enabled her to compensate for the limitations of ageing. Young people were attracted to her because of her benevolent warmth and motherliness, so she had little time to feel lonely or alone.

The old age I have just described may well be that of a fortunate woman who has successfully adapted to the traumatic losses and natural crises of a normal life cycle. She has come to terms with the daydreams of youth, which life has not fulfilled, and considers that she has had a good-enough life which helps her to enjoy a serene old age.

For other women, old age may be a time for anger and impotent rage at what has not been fulfilled in the past and never will be in the future. The painful phrase 'Never more' may ring in a woman's mind and give her no peace as she feels the doors of life gradually closing in upon her and her aspirations. Yet even at this late stage, therapy may help a woman actively to resume her life as a vigorous sexual person rather than confine herself to daydreams and night dreams.

Mrs O came into therapy in her late fifties, following her husband's death. She felt devastated by this event, since not only was she now a widow and alone, but she had also lost the high professional status that his work had brought her. This final loss had been the last of a lifelong series of losses. As a child she was evacuated to America during the War, and an emotional reunion with her mother had not been successful when she returned. She

174

disliked her mother and felt that she could not regain the early close tie with her, since another baby had been born in her absence. Her mother's strict rules about her feminine role and her sexuality did not coincide with her own. She felt enraged with her mother and could not use her good mind to study, since it was blocked by anger. She left England to live and work abroad. Away from her mother and her mother's country, she succeeded in doing well professionally and in enjoying a sexual life, which she felt her mother had never given her permission to do. In due course she married and had children, whom she loved, but the marriage was unhappy and her husband fled to his own country, taking the children with him. Mrs O was devastated and remained in part psychically dead, as if the loss of her children was a punishment for the sexual activity her mother had forbidden. She felt that she would never recover. During the course of her therapy Mrs O worked through the earlier problems of separation from her mother, and the rage and frustration that pervaded their relationship as well as their love. They gradually recovered the happier relationship of her earlier years. Most of this work was achieved by the working-through in analysis of the difficulties in their relationship. The careful monitoring of transference and countertrans-ference phenomena, reflections of her troubled internal world, led to a more mature relationship between mother and daughter. Therapy helped Mrs O to regain her sense of self-esteem and attractiveness. She met a man who pleased her, and whom she pleased. Their affair helped her to reaffirm her identity both as an attractive sexual woman and as a dearly loved child, which had been undermined by the unresolved tragedies, losses and sepa-rations of her early life.

*

Margaret Mahler, whose seminal work on the infant's separation and individuation from the mother has helped our understanding of the psychological birth of each individual, writes: 'Our life course is characterized by a simultaneous and continual distancing from the all-good symbiotic mother who represents our desire for what we fantasize was an originally blissful state of oneness.' For many old people death may in fantasy be a psychological reunion with the mother, and a return to the safety of her womb. Birth and death are closely linked in the unconscious, for we cannot intellectually grasp the notion of nonexistence. Marcel Proust's emotional separation from his mother seemed to be an inconsolable loss until, in his last book, he wrote that now he recognized that at the end of his life what he had been seeking for all along was what he had had at the beginning. That longing for an all-powerful, protective and loving figure is something we never outgrow and unconsciously seek in our adult relationships.

Mrs P, a woman in her late seventies who had always lived her life to the full, had identified with her beautiful mother not only by marrying and bearing children but also by encouraging numerous male admirers to cluster around her. She returned to therapy because she was in conflict about her latest lover, who was many years younger than she was. This embarrassed her, because his body looked younger than her own. What became clear as our work progressed was that in their lovemaking, not only was he the potent lover who deeply satisfied her adult self and helped her to deny ageing and death, but the affectionate foreplay between them unconsciously recalled her mother's delight in her little daughter's body. Thus the pre-oedipal satisfaction of the loving bodily

176

relationship between her mother and herself was refound in this last adult sexual relationship. The wheel had come full circle, since unconsciously Mrs P regained the early bodily pleasures with her mother which she had consciously forgotten.

Many women who have had more tranquil, satisfying lives themselves may find it difficult to identify with the patients I have described. They are fortunate. However, my observations are based on listening carefully to my older women patients who have experienced difficulties in their lives, and have come for psychoanalytic help in order to ease their pain and to help them live their lives to the full. One is not less of a woman if youth and the child-bearing years have passed.

WORKING WITH WOMEN SURVIVORS OF THE HOLOCAUST:

Affective Experiences in Transference and Countertransference*

For young women who had survived the concentration camps, the longing to become pregnant and the wish to bring a new life into a world no longer dominated by sadism and psychic death were overwhelming. Babies for these women were an important concrete manifestation of the restoration of normality from a psychotic world and the re-establishment of family life that had been destroyed. Infertility, painful as it is for most women, was almost unbearable for them, since the next generation also concretely replaced those who had been killed and enabled the survivors to avoid the recognition of loss and of mourning.

Hopelessness and psychic surrender to an unbearable

* Presented at the 34th International Psychoanalytical Congress, Hamburg, July 1985, and published in *International Journal of Psycho-Analysis* (1986) 67: 295–306.

situation were counteracted by the hope of giving birth to a healthy child and, in mothering it, recovering some of the normal pleasures of life that the mother herself had been robbed of. Unconsciously, pregnancy afforded these young women two aspects of emotional identification: with the omnipotent, life-giving pre-oedipal mother they had lost, based on a biological foundation, and also with the foetus, as if it represented themselves as baby and as child (Pines, 1982).

Yet one of the tasks of mothering is also to facilitate the child's healthy drive towards separation and individuation. Adolescence, an important stage in the life cycle when the healthy child must finally separate from her parents, take responsibility for her own body and her sexuality and often physically leave the parents' home to pursue her own life, is an equally important stage of the life cycle for the parents. Most analysts are familiar with the pain and mourning at this stage experienced by mothers who have been closely invested in their children's lives. The psychologically healthier the child, the stronger her rebellion must be, and the more painful to her mother must be the temporary loss of the loving closeness. Painful as the mourning must be for her, it may lead to a positive increase in psychic freedom and further developments in her own life.

In this paper I wish to describe and discuss the effect of this normal transitional crisis upon two women, one of whom I have known for nearly thirty years, first as her physician and later as her analyst. Both were survivors of Auschwitz. Both would have seemed to have made an impressive recovery from their traumatic earlier situations, to have worked, married and successfully brought up children whom they enjoyed. Yet it was at this stage that the effects of their previous tragedies became overwhelming and made them seek psychotherapeutic help from me. It was as if their adaptation to life after the war had collapsed with their children's separation from them and the parting of the secure world of mother and child. They could no longer identify with their children, live through and for them, and substitute them for those who had been lost. They were now forced to face the destruction of their previous world, to attempt to come to terms with the violent deaths of important figures in that world, to mourn them and to face the guilt of their own survival.

Psychoanalytic Understanding of the Trauma of Survivors and Its After-Effects

Psychoanalytical studies, notably by Krystal and his co-authors (1968), Krystal and Niederland (1971), Krystal (1971, 1974, 1975, 1977), have focused upon the after-effects of catastrophic trauma on survivors. The effects of the Holocaust upon the second generation have been studied by a group led by Jocovy and Kestenberg (1982). Grubrich-Simitis, in two notable papers, has described the predicament of the survivor and her children in which concrete thought results from their blocking of emotions and denial of experiences and leads to their inability to use metaphor (1984).

It is generally agreed that there is a 'psychic closing off' (Lifton, 1967) in survivors, many of whom have experienced 'the Mussulman stage' in the camps where the victim's emotional and physical strength had been eroded. Their state corresponds to the definition of trauma described by Anna Freud (1967): 'shattering, devastating, causing internal disruption by putting ego function mediation out of action'. Krystal (1974) concludes that the final common path of traumatization was the development of overwhelming affects, as Freud had indicated originally.

180

Krystal first describes the manifestations of a continued state of constriction of mental functions and episodic freezing in which the individual becomes ineffective in the presence of a dominating person – that is to say, a repetition of the surrender position; secondly, the continuing capacity of memory fragments to evoke intense affects, a regression in cognitive and expressive affects leading to psychosomatic disorders, a general impairment of fantasy life (corresponding to the *pensée opératoire* described by Marty and de M'Uzan, 1963).

Grubrich-Simitis (1984) describes the emotional strain on the analyst in working with children of survivors from the Holocaust. In her view: 'of decisive importance for the patient in this stage of the analysis seems to be the emotional perception of the analyst's feelings'. She calls this the phase of joint acceptance of the Holocaust reality. (See also Gyomroi, 1963.)

The Clinical Material

These *sequelae* were present in varying degrees in both my patients. I shall, however, focus upon the concrete nature of the material, their somatization of psychic pain in order to avoid overwhelming and unbearable emotional affects, and my use of the real relationship with them as well as the affective experience of the countertransference in order to facilitate the analytic work. Since dreaming was intolerable to these patients because of their fear of what would be remembered or affectively re-experienced, the countertransference became one of the most effective analytic tools. The patients either avoided sleep until they were totally exhausted or took powerful hypnotics which made them unable to remember their dreams.

I first met Mrs B when I was a young physician. Very little was known at the time about the emotional impact of the Holocaust upon the survivors. Mrs B developed a very positive transference towards me, since in my caring for her body she could safely regress and re-experience the most primitive form of maternal care.

Mrs B was a strikingly beautiful young blonde woman when we first met. She had spent her adolescence in Auschwitz, and came to England after her release. She had married a kind but passive man, but his relatively impotent sexuality did not disturb her, since she herself was frigid. She was desperate to have a child and became pregnant several times, but miscarried each time. Each miscarriage was almost unbearably painful psychically, since she longed to have a child. After each miscarriage she took a long time to recover physically and would remain huddled in bed under the covers in a darkened room, with no apparent physical cause for this state. I was puzzled, but did not understand at that time. Her family, all of whom were survivors, would anxiously look after her and were very supportive to her. This was a repetition of her childhood situation when she had been the pretty, ill child of the family. Her fragility had made her father and her siblings very protective towards her, and it was the only time that her cold but dutiful mother showed her any physical care. Illness brought her a secondary gain, since she could regress to being a child, and let another woman touch her and soothe her pain. In my view, she avoided hopeless despair by finding a psychosomatic solution to psychic pain, and regained the most primitive form of maternal comfort. In this way she repeated her infantile experience of a mother who could care for her body but not for her feelings (Pines, 1980).

Eventually Mrs B succeeded in bearing several girl children. The first child was named after her dead mother and was the object of Mrs B's ambivalence. The child was meticulously cared for physically and dressed like a little

182

doll. Yet when she was normally disobedient Mrs B would react with unaccustomed fury, or at other times sit upon her lap as if she were the baby and her own child was the mother. This was unusual, since Mrs B was invariably kind and generous to everyone she came in contact with. Her child reacted with signs of extreme anxiety, and after some time in psychotherapy with a colleague she settled down into being a docile, good daughter who still looks after her mother when she is ill, as if she were mother to her own mother. Mrs B's daughter is now married with four children. No plastic bag is allowed into her house, since her constant anxiety is that one of her children may accidentally suffocate by playfully placing it over his head. Neither she nor her mother has any insight into what might have been transmitted by her mother's Holocaust experience.

The youngest daughter was always much less docile and in many ways was over-indulged by her mother as if, through her, she was able to express the anger and rebelliousness that would have led to death in the camp. She grew into a rebellious, demanding adolescent. Her intellectual and sexual frustration, since she could not allow herself normal flirtatiousness in this rigid home setting, was acted out by furious verbal attacks on her mother, who masochistically submitted. Much of her rage was motivated by envy of her mother's outstanding physical beauty which none of her daughters could match. Unconsciously, her anger was also an attempt to separate emotionally from her mother, who lived through her. This child thus became a terrifying aggressor to whom her mother passively and silently submitted. Eventually a suitable young husband was found for the girl, who fell head over heels in love with him.

After the wedding Mrs B fell into a state of hopelessness. She had suddenly lost her last child and witnessed her daughter's obvious sexual satisfaction with her new husband, a state that overwhelmed her mother with envy and rage. Mrs B's husband was impotent and passive. She had always resisted other men's sexual attraction towards her, but she suddenly succumbed to an old friend, who had always pursued her. Tormented by her guilt and her envy of her daughter, she recognized that she was on the verge of a breakdown, that her sexual acting-out could not relieve her, and came to me for help.

It was on the basis of a longstanding feeling of basic trust in me that Mrs B could enter analysis and face the daunting task of re-experiencing affectively and sharing with me her tragic past that she could not master on her own. It was equally on the basis of a long relationship with Mrs B that I felt that I must not fail her, although I did not know then what an affective emotional strain my countertransference would be.

Mrs B revealed a totally different aspect of herself when we began analysis. The gentle, kind woman I had known was replaced by an implacably cruel, authoritarian figure, striding round my consulting room, towering over me in my chair, and overpowering my sense of my analytic self. I had become the victim of a merciless persecutor in someone I had hitherto regarded as familiar and friendly. I was filled with overwhelming feelings of helpless despair from which I felt I could not escape.[1] I later understood that this was a reversal of Mrs B's experience in the Holocaust, and a violent projection into me of affects that she had split off and denied at a cost to her psychic health. It was also the first overt manifestation of a hidden identification with the aggressor that emerged into consciousness as the analysis proceeded. Mrs B had been brought up in a country village where Jews and non-Jews had lived side by side for many generations. When her country was invaded, her familiar childhood friends

184

became persecutors who denounced her and her family to the SS, although physically they could all have passed for non-Jews since they were tall, blond and blue-eyed.

Mrs B told me that her father had been the warm parent of her childhood, whereas her cold and dutiful mother could show her physical affection only when she was ill – hence in the previous transference to me as her physician she had recaptured the one experience in which her mother's touch showed her bodily love for her. Frequently Mrs B had shared her parents' bed when she was ill, and lay cuddled against her father, although he always insisted that she must lie with her back to him. Although she had no conscious memory of the parental intercourse, it became clear that the primal-scene material had influenced her infantile sexuality and her fantasy life. For example, when she had been ill in her own bed she was frequently enuretic, thus unconsciously identifying with the paternal role in the primal scene.

Her adolescence began with her first menstrual period a week before the family was sent to Auschwitz. In the shadow of death neither her period nor her enuresis occurred in the camp. Mrs B recalled her father cuddling her closely as they travelled in the train to Auschwitz. Protected by him, she felt in a dreamlike state in which neither her own terror nor that of others could affectively touch her. On arrival at Auschwitz she was forcibly torn from her father's arms and never saw him again. She was driven into a room filled with women, including her mother and sister. There she suddenly saw a beautiful dark-haired man, immaculately dressed, who selected her mother, her sister and herself for the working living and not for death. Later she learned that he was Dr Mengele, the Angel of Death of Auschwitz. Although she never saw him again, his beautiful appearance remained in her adolescent mind. In the camp Mrs B, overwhelmed by physical and emotional helplessness and despair, almost reached a state of psychic death. Supported physically and emotionally by both her mother and her sister until her mother's death, Mrs B survived eventually through her sister's devoted care.

The first stage of Mrs B's analysis was a testing time for us both. Not only did Mrs B need to test my capacity to hold her, and enable her to live, as her sister had done; she also needed to test my capacity to express her affects for her until she was strong enough to feel them herself. My countertransference was emotionally strenuous, and at times almost unbearable, but I was sustained by the relationship that had existed between us for many years and my knowledge of another aspect of Mrs B. This was the phase of joint acceptance of the Holocaust reality defined by Grubrich-Simitis (1984). Once she had tested me enough and could appreciate my capacity to hold her in the transference as her mother and sister had done in Auschwitz, Mrs B could lie on the couch, enter into full analysis and accept the impact of affective responses that she had never been in touch with before. Many times she verbalized my own feeling that it was so painful that she wished she had never begun, yet she also knew that she would never be well if she did not go on. As her ego strengthened she recovered her own affective responses, the strain on my countertransference diminished and a more classical form of analysis ensued.

It became clear that Mrs B had always lived in a double reality (Kestenberg, 1982): that of the camp and that of her present life. Lying in bed with the curtains drawn had concretely repeated her life in the camp. Neither fantasy nor dreaming was available to her for relief or mastery. Watching her children run naked before her into the bathroom, it was as if she again watched other children running to the gas chamber at Auschwitz.

The massive traumatization she had experienced as an adolescent had damaged her ego in terms of affective and symbolic functions, and in the perception of the passage of time. Now holiday breaks involving separation became difficult for her to bear, and she relived much of her traumatic past affectively. At times she had to run out of shops crowded with people because she felt she was suffocating and had an impulse to climb up the walls to get air as the people in the gas chamber had done. Mrs B had in fact once been rescued from the gas chamber barracks by a woman *kapo* with whom her mother and sister had pleaded. It was as if the holiday break re-enacted her fantasy of the gas chamber from which I was to rescue her, but in which I could also put her as if I were the persecuting *kapo*. Mrs B could sleep only with the aid of heavy hypnotics.

As our work proceeded, Mrs B recovered her beauty and her self-confidence in her sexual attraction. She became overtly angry and contemptuous of the dark-haired psychiatrist who had referred her to me when he reduced the frequency of her visits to him because she was better. It was as if her transference towards him repeated her feelings of humiliation: that however beautiful her adolescent body had become she could not deny the reality of the parental bed, nor had the Angel of Death preferred her to her mother and sister. In a slip she called her psychiatrist 'Dr Mengele'.

Analysis of this material enabled us to understand that the primary male object, her father, had been split into the good man who cuddled her and protected her, as her husband did, and the terrifying father of the primal scene who humiliated women and sadistically attacked their bodies, represented by Dr Mengele. Mrs B dreamed that a woman looking like herself gave her a book entitled *The Joy of Sex*, and was greatly relieved by this dream. It was at this time that she visited her eldest brother's wife, who has been perpetually ill since she was released from Auschwitz. As she looked at her sister-in-law's ill face, Mrs B described her immediate reaction of feeling psychically dead again, as she had felt in the camp. The deadness masked the final triumph of her own survival over her rejecting mother, which had been repeated with me at the beginning of her analysis and defended her from the knowledge of her own infantile sadistic impulses towards her mother which had been so dramatically acted out by others in Auschwitz. Mrs B's strengthened ego and the therapeutic alliance between us enabled her to accept these interpretations of her conflicts and avoid withdrawing into psychic deadness or masochistic self-punishment. Several dreams following this work revealed the revival of Mrs B's unresolved oedipal drama that had occurred with her daughter's adolescent sexuality. In each dream she triumphed over her daughter by being the sexual woman whom her admirers preferred, and in each dream the young man resembled her father, the psychiatrist or Dr Mengele. It became clear that in her childhood Mrs B had used her illness in order to interrupt the parental intercourse, and had felt triumphant at her secret success.

At this stage Mrs B felt acutely sexually frustrated by her husband. Several times she dreamed of being penetrated by a large penis, and was awakened by strong orgasmic feelings. A surprising new development occurred. The black chauffeur who drove her to her analytic sessions became her secret lover. A rented flat provided them with a secret domestic setting in which Mrs B cooked for him and also became his sexual partner. She was deeply satisfied by his potency, whilst I silently experienced feelings of anxiety about his potential sadism and violence, affects she did not appear to feel despite some of his behaviour towards her. Gradually the balance

188

between them changed. It became clear that a repressed fantasy about the Black Angel of Auschwitz had forced its way into consciousness and was compulsively acted out. Her lover now became her helpless victim and she became his oppressor. Her sadistic triumph was acted out by a reversal of roles in which she would sexually excite him in foreplay but refuse him penetration, thus controlling his orgasmic response and castrating him. She tamed his violence by her conscious sweetness and physical care for him, defensive measures against her own aggressive castration wishes, which she denied.

It became clear that the sexual game which she compulsively played with potential violence and death was also an attempt to control physical danger and save her life. In this way she attempted to master her catastrophic helplessness in the camp. This behaviour, an identification with the aggressor, could not be contained within the transference, since bodily danger and bodily satisfaction were essential components of her drama. In my view the concrete acting-out of her sexual fantasies was not a resistance to analysis but an essential working-through of her traumatic past that had been facilitated by analysis.

It followed that in the transference our roles became reversed as I silently experienced affects of anxiety about this man's potential violence and Mrs B's physical danger, as if I had been the helpless child Mrs B had been in her parents' bed, the anonymous spectator described by McDougall (1972). This dangerous game was not only an attempt to actualize and act out the adolescent fantasy about the Black Angel of Auschwitz and master the helplessness of the camp, but contained the underlying experiences and fantasies of the primal scene. It was psychologically preferable to the state of aphanasis and psychic death in which she had existed for so long. In addition I was made to experience affectively the horrifying aspects of Mrs B's sadism that she had to split off or project in order to act out some of her perverse use of her sexual partner. Perversion and sadism had been so rampant in the psychotic world of the camp that Mrs B had found it impossible to accept these aspects in herself.

Mrs B's sexual affair ended as suddenly as it had begun. It was as if the sexual game she had acted out had not only reactivated and worked through the forbidden wishes and fantasies of her childhood but restored her sense of her adult identity. She was able to mourn the death of her family and to use her new-found capacity to be creative. In mourning her dead family Mrs B, who had never written anything before, wrote a touching book recalling her childhood, her happy life in her native village, her experiences in the Holocaust in which so many people she loved had been killed. It was as if mourning them enabled her to bring them to life in her book. Mrs B now lives as a wife, mother and grandmother, but has never written anything else. She no longer lives in a double reality, but her traumatic past can never be forgotten, despite the analysis of her internal conflicts.

The second patient, Mrs C, was referred to me following a serious suicidal attempt for which she had been hospitalized and received ECT treatment.

Mrs C's childhood had been difficult. She was born posthumously, some months after her father's death. Her mother had immediately married again. Her stepfather proved to be mentally unstable, subject to outbursts of irrational rage, but was always loving and kind to his little stepdaughter. Her strict, toothless, maternal grandmother took care of her and brought her up to be a very good, obedient, clean child. Mrs C's mother worked hard as a dressmaker to earn their living. She showed no overt physical affection to her child but made her beautiful clothes which the little girl coquettishly modelled for her admiring audience of sewing-girls, mother and grand-mother. She was a pretty, clever little girl, doing well at school, a good performer, always entertaining and singing. However, when overwhelmed by frustration, anger or despair – feelings which were not acceptable to her mother and grandmother, for whom she had to be a pretty, well-dressed little doll – Mrs C would run to the cemetery and cry to her father's tombstone. In her fantasy her father was with God, looking down upon her, accepting the feelings that could not be accepted at home, and protect-ing her. She married young and moved away to escape her parents' quarrels and the shame of her stepfather's increasingly obvious illness.

Despite the fact that in their brief year of marriage she and her husband had to share her mother-in-law's bed-room, Mrs C allowed her young husband to enjoy her body, and once experienced orgasm. When he was drafted, Mrs C, who had been a hardworking and valued employee, was kept on at her job until Jews were ordered into ghettos. Thus she had had time to learn to know her own strength before she was sent to Auschwitz. She also learned to live solitarily and hidden, but to function independently. Perhaps her hard childhood had made her strong. Mrs B had not reached this stage in the life cycle before overwhelming calamity struck.

When Mrs C's benevolent employer dared keep her no longer, she returned to join her parents in the ghetto. She was unable to stand her father's psychosis and parents' constant quarrelling, and went to live with her aunt. She has never forgiven herself for not travelling to Auschwitz with her mother and dying with her, despite all rational knowledge that the old were separated from the young on arrival, and killed. On arrival at Auschwitz, Mrs C was hit on the jaw by one of the guards, and since then she has had recurrent dental pain. X-rays have shown that she may have incurred a minor fracture, but therapy has shown the deeper psychic significance of her physical pain. In Auschwitz, Mrs C retained part of her observing ego, which enabled her to avoid the psychic death to which Mrs B succumbed. She preserved her sense of self by continuing to be a hardworking young woman, compliant to anyone in authority, and having one close friend who mothered her and whom she mothered. Above all, she remained clean and tidy by exchanging her precious crust of bread for clean camp clothes whenever they were issued. However, she felt dead. Anger, despair or anguish were affectively avoided in this way, although she occasionally pleaded to her father when she looked up at the sky. But she now had to accept the passing of her childhood fantasy that either he or God could rescue her.

Mrs C thus survived Auschwitz, where her parents and most of her family and friends had perished. After her liberation she made her way back to her home town, hoping that her young husband would be there. As the survivors drifted back to the town, Mrs C, after some time, consciously had to accept his loss, and that she would have to find another man to father the child she yearned for. She was extremely pretty and popular, and eventually married a man who had lost his first wife and child. She chose him for his solidity and physical courage, and most of all for his capacity to be a strong paternal figure. One child, a son, was born to them. She told me later, 'I lost myself in Auschwitz', and indeed this was psychically true, since she continued to exist as a hardworking, ambitious wife and mother, but to live affectively through her cherished only child. Her son was a premature, fragile infant whom Mrs C nursed devotedly, as if she were also symbolically bringing the dead back to life.

Her son thus unconsciously became a substitute for her idealized first husband.

When a revolution took place after a further invasion of their country, Mrs C and her family escaped to England. Mrs C continued to function as a hardworking model employee at work, entertaining and lively socially, and in addition devoting herself to keeping her home, her husband, and her son and herself meticulously clean. In particular, all their clothes were freshly laundered every day, as if this concretely reminded her that they were not in the camp.

Mrs C broke down when her son decided to make an early marriage to a non-Jewish English girl. For her, it was as if she had not kept her debt to her murdered family. It was as if she could not now, through her son, replace those who had died. She became severely depressed and suffered from unbearable pain in her jaw and in her upper teeth. Most of her healthy teeth had been extracted by an incompetent dentist, but the pain had not diminished. Mrs C had submitted without any protest to her dentist's rough treatment and tried to wear a denture, which again caused her acute pain. In her analysis we understood the underlying emotional experience that was contained in her dental pain.

Following this Mrs C made a serious suicide attempt, was hospitalized and treated by ECT. Later she was referred to me.

Our work together was not founded upon a real relationship where basic trust had been established for many years, and the beginning of her analysis was therefore markedly different from that of the analysis with Mrs B. Mrs C, a petite, extremely attractive and well-groomed woman who looked much younger than her age, always came to her sessions accompanied by a male friend who left her and came to fetch her again. It took some months for her to feel sufficiently secure in her therapeutic alliance with me to be able to come to her sessions unaccompanied. There could be no sexual relationship with her friend, since he was impotent, but he was protective and kindly towards her. Mrs C's husband was not allowed to bring her and fetch her. Later in her analysis we understood the significance of this concrete embodiment of a second man.

Mrs C could never lie on the couch and would sit opposite me, watching my face intently as I reacted to her story. I learned then that to read an account of Auschwitz was affectively very different from being in the living presence of a survivor. My natural empathy towards a woman whose life had contained so much pain, and so much strength at the same time, enabled me to accept Mrs C's structuring of the analytic setting and not to regard it as a resistance that must be overcome in the interests of working through some of her problems. My affective response to her narrative, which she herself spoke calmly, as if it had happened to someone else, was difficult to bear. At times I felt sadness and pity, or I experienced horror and anger at the senseless destruction of her world and the dehumanization and humiliation of the camp. Yet I was not totally or helplessly overwhelmed by my experience, as I had been made to be with Mrs B, and I could retain my analytic self, as Mrs C had retained some of her observing ego in the camp.

We later acknowledged together that unless Mrs C had first tested my ability to express affectively that which she could not allow herself to do, and had concretely seen my affective response as well as my capacity to bear the situation, she would not have continued to come. What seemed to be resistance was, in effect, the beginning phase of her therapy. Classical analytic work with the interpretation of unconscious material, wishes and fantasies, as well as the work in the transference, proved to be impossible at that time. My acceptance of the reality of the Holocaust was essential before any therapeutic alliance could develop or any attempt could be made to interpret and work through some of the underlying conflicts.

Mrs C avoided dreaming. She either stayed up all night, rearranging her drawers in her bedroom or playing with the ornaments as if she were a little girl; or she took heavy hypnotics which crashed her into a dreamless sleep. It was as if dreaming, recollection, and its accompanying affective response would overwhelm her and must be avoided at any cost. Yet since therapy necessitates the re-experience of affects in the transference, it was through the affective experience of the countertransference that our major work was done at this stage. It was as if Mrs C repeated one of the earliest experiences of the mother–infant relationship in which an empathic mother contains the infant's affective distress and gives it meaning before it becomes totally overwhelmed. It was therefore upon the maternal aspect of my countertransference that Mrs C drew.

It became clear that unconsciously some of the aspects of her traumatic camp life were repeated in her second marriage. Her husband was put into the position of being the Nazi master while she remained his hardworking, compliant slave. Mrs C accepted my interpretations of the projection of her traumatic inner reality on to her present reality and object relationships. It was as if psychically she was still in the camp, with an accompanying regression of affective experience, somatization and timeless concrete thought. Yet she was impressively pretty, well-groomed and well-dressed, no matter how psychically distressed she felt. It became clear that she cared for her body in the way that her mother had cared for it in her childhood. It was as if her own body still belonged to her mother and was unconsciously her well-tended memorial, since she had no concrete inheritance from her and no tombstone to visit. Since her body unconsciously belonged to her mother, she became frigid after her son was born.

As this material was worked through, Mrs C's ego strengthened considerably. She could safely allow herself to experience her own anger – with her son in particular for betraying her – since I was there to hold her analytically. She no longer feared that she would be helplessly overwhelmed and psychically destroyed for her anger. The projections on to her husband and her son diminished, since they no longer represented the persecuting guards of Auschwitz. Just as she accepted her anger with them, she could also now gain access to her natural generosity and love towards them as separate objects rather than living through them. Somatization of her psychic pain diminished, and she allowed herself to find a new dentist who gave her considerable relief and pulled no more teeth. Acceptance of her parents' unknown deaths involved mourning those figures belonging to the past and an acceptance of the passage of time. Our work came to a fixed termination date, and in her last session Mrs C reported her first dream, which she had had the night before. In the dream she was in the camp again, standing in line with others, dressed in her camp clothes. The SS officer inspecting his prisoners said to her, 'If you can stand the pain, you can live'. Another SS guard approached her as she opened her mouth, put in a large forceps and brutally wrenched out a tooth. The pain was almost unbearable but she stood it without a murmur, and was allowed to live. Since it was our last session, the dream could not be worked through, but it became clear that the price she paid for survival was bodily damage and pain.[2]

For the next five years Mrs C came to see me from time to time. To her great joy, two little granddaughters were born and grew to be pretty little girls, as she had been.

196

She was able to work successfully in her husband's prosperous business, she slept fairly well, her denture fitted and she had very little pain. Mr and Mrs C led an active social life and travelled abroad on holiday, including several trips back to their country of origin. Mrs C, who had always longed to return to her roots, now accepted that her life was in England, and felt it to be home, where her new family was.

Unexpectedly, Mrs C returned to see me in despair. Two major calamities had befallen her. Her son had suddenly left his wife and children and decided to divorce because of his wife's difficult character. For Mrs C, the little family that had been gradually rebuilt was shattered again. She felt overwhelming rage towards her son, as if he were not only the destroyer of her new world but also represented those who had first destroyed it. His divorce made her feel ashamed, as though it repeated her childhood experience of feeling ashamed about her stepfather's humiliating psychotic behaviour. Yet she was also in touch with his unhappiness and could not attack him. She again became intensely depressed, suicidal and self-destructive, as if in this way she attempted to spare him by turning her rage against herself. The second calamity was the unexpected death of her trusted dentist at this stressful time. Mrs C was angered at his abandonment of her, but also loyal to him, since no other dentist was allowed to help her.

Our previous work and the strong therapeutic alliance we had formed enabled her to expose herself to me without shame. This time, Mrs C was in touch with her own affects which were experienced in the session. My counter-transference, whilst empathic to her further experiences of loss and pain, was not as stressful as it once had been and I could return to a more detached analytic stance. Mrs C no longer watched my face for my response or needed me to feel her affects for her. She could now verbalize her own and receive some comfort from my response, since I was not the silent, dead, punitive father to whom she had previously turned, nor the silent god who had abandoned her in Auschwitz.

As the themes of rejection, shame and humiliation were worked through, Mrs C recovered some of her previous equilibrium and, in particular, a stronger sense of self-esteem. At this time she was admitted to hospital for a minor operation. When she was heavily sedated, a nurse opened her door and said, 'Number Twenty, have you taken your pills?' Enraged and humiliated by this, as if she were again being treated as a nameless number in camp, Mrs C got out of bed and staggered upstairs to the Sister's desk, where the nurse was standing. She said with dignity, 'I am no longer a number. I have a name, and it is Mrs C.' It was clear that her self-esteem and her sense of time had been restored, that the camp was now to some degree in the past and no longer her present reality.

Following this event we entered a new phase of her therapy. Mrs C felt closely identified with her fatherless granddaughters and made strenuous efforts to recover them. Despite her daughter-in-law's bitterness and anger towards her, Mrs C stood firm and did not submit to her as she once had done. It became clear that Mrs C's wish to rescue her grandchildren also contained her childhood longing to be rescued herself. For the first time she remembered that when she had helped her mother to calm her stepfather in one of his mad rages by putting wet sheets over him while he lay in bed, she had had an almost overwhelming impulse to stuff them into his mouth and choke him to stop his shouting. Thus her childhood murderous wishes towards him, which had been split off and repressed, had been fulfilled by the gas chambers.

Following this memory, Mrs C began to mourn for her

parents' death and the destruction of her world. It was then that she dreamed the second dream of her therapy. In her dream, she was sitting on a stone by the roadside in her native country. She looked her present age. She saw a man, dressed in a pre-war suit, walking towards her, carrying a bundle on his back. As he passed he turned his head towards her and she saw that it was her first husband, looking the same age as she now was. She jumped up and ran to him, but he angrily hit her on her jaw where she has the pain, and walked away. She did not care about the pain and ran after him, crying his name. She was so happy to have seen him that she sat up in her kitchen all night, as if she had recovered him within herself. Thus we could see that his loss had felt like an angry, painful blow to her, and that in fantasy he had always been in her mind, and had aged with her. Mrs C's body and her sexuality still unconsciously belonged to her first husband, whose death had never been confirmed. Mourning his loss could now begin.

Mrs C was forced to consult a new dentist. At her first appointment she felt unbearable pain when he touched her and screamed, 'I want my mother!' Overwhelmed by her intense feelings of loss, pain and deprivation, Mrs C wept continuously for many days, something she had never allowed herself to do before. She reflected bitterly that throughout her life she had been cheated of normal happiness, although she had always tried to be a good and dutiful person.

Mrs C's therapy was an intense emotional strain both for her and for her analyst, and it would have been satisfying to be able to report that working-through had brought her a great deal of relief. This is not the case. As she ages, Mrs C still remains in public the lively, pretty woman that she can be. Her body is very nicely cared for, and she is well groomed and well dressed. But she withdraws from the social world, and the somatization of her psychic pain has returned. She no longer works or travels, and her dental pain flares up when she is emotionally stressed. She comes to see me from time to time, but tries to avoid repeating intense affects. I feel that I have helped her to exist but not to live again, and we share a feeling of resignation.[3]

Conclusion

I have described some late after-effects of massive traumatization in two women survivors of the Holocaust. Both appeared to have functioned relatively well after their release until their children became adolescent and separated from them. This essentially normal stage of the life cycle led to a breakdown in their apparent adaptation to life, since mourning the separation from their children forced them to face the destruction of their previous world, the separation from important figures, murdered and as yet unmourned, and the guilt of their own survival. Disturbances of affective and cognitive functions – the use of concrete thinking as opposed to metaphor, a regression in the expression of affect, a non-differentiation of psychic and somatic pain – have been described by many observers, notably Krystal. All these symptoms were present in both my patients in varying degrees. Neither of them had shared their Holocaust experiences with their children, or ever talked about them before.

Denial, repression and splitting had resulted in a state of concretism, severely impaired fantasy life, and a return to a state of psychic death in order to avoid overwhelming and unbearably painful feelings. This reversion to concrete thought also influenced the beginning of the analysis, since metaphor was unavailable. The task of working through the patients' unbearable experiences and the recovery of affects in the analytic setting evoked an unbearable countertransference. Yet it seemed to be an inevitable and necessary part of the patients' preparations for analytic work that they both needed to test the analyst's strength and capacity to withstand the haunting horror that they themselves had avoided by denial and splitting. The deep feelings of insecurity and destruction of basic trust engendered in these patients by their Holocaust experience contributed to the initial difficulty of maintaining a classical analytic technique for patient and analyst alike. Indeed, the painful countertransference feelings of shock and deep despair at man's inhumanity to man frequently evoked a strong desire to distance the patient emotionally, and to avoid the analytic empathy and understanding that are essential to the working-through of the patient's problems. Yet in the absence of dreams and fantasy life in the patients' material, it was only through the acceptance and careful monitoring of the countertransference that their denial of their own affects could be given up and their haunting double reality shared.

It was to Mrs B's advantage that her basic trust in my ability to help her psychic pain was based upon a success-ful doctor–patient relationship. Such a long-established relationship would in my view normally prove to be a contra-indication to analytic work, since it might well distort both transference and countertransference. Never-theless her long-established trust in me, and my accept-ance of responsibility for her, enabled us both to plunge immediately into the concrete reality that could no longer be repressed after her last child's marriage. Analysis, in my view, enabled Mrs B to acknowledge her intense sexual frustration, to bring into consciousness a long-repressed compulsive sexual fantasy which could be worked through only after it had been externalized and the sexual frustration satisfied through concrete bodily experience. In my opinion this was not resistance to a transference but a non-verbal communication which I had to acknowledge and tolerate, and which eventually led to mourning and creativity.

Mrs B does not appear to have repeated a similar sexual episode. Although her sexual fantasy contained elements of sadomasochistic primal-scene fantasies, these were reinforced by an adolescence spent in a world where intense sadomasochistic fantasies were concretely enacted as part of daily life. The adolescent process, with its stimulus towards genital sexuality, pushed Mrs B into a further identification with the powerful sadistic aggressor in the camp to whom her mother, her sister and she herself had helplessly to submit. Turning the passive into the active became the means of reversing her humiliation in the safety of the holding environment which her analysis provided. Mrs B appears to have come to terms, as far as is humanly possible, with her past traumatic experiences, and uses her further identification with her analyst to be a strong friend to others who are in need. The question to which I do not know the answer is whether her sadomasochistic identifications have been modified and worked through or have again been split off and repressed, and are in danger of reappearing under the pressure of further life events.

Mrs C, the second patient, had entered into a post-adolescent phase of marriage and satisfactory sexuality before her Holocaust experience. A difficult childhood in which she had learned to look after herself enabled her to continue to maintain herself in the camp, to survive revolution after her release, and emigration to a new country. Nevertheless, the price she paid for her survival was somatization of pain and masochistic submission to dental ill-treatment. Hidden behind her masochistic submission to somatic pain, which she could not relinquish, was despair and guilt at surviving her husband and her parents. Anger was avoided at all costs, for rage in the camp would inevitably have led to death. Mrs C concretely protected others from her rage by making her bite harmless and turning her rage against herself; or she projected her sadism into others, rather than consciously accepting it in herself as an identification with the aggressor in the camp. However, Mrs C's sadism was unconsciously a powerful means of causing those who cared for her – including her doctors and her analyst – to suffer and feel guilty, since they could not relieve her. Nevertheless, after some time, when basic trust in her analyst and her dentist was established, Mrs C could acknowledge her fury with those who had murdered the ones she had loved and cheated her of her youth. She enjoyed family, work and life until further blows of fate ended in the dispersal of the new family she had enjoyed, and with the sudden death of her beloved dentist. As Mrs C aged it was as if she could no longer imagine that life could be generous after so much pain and loss before and after the camp, or enable her to make a new family to replace the one she had lost. Nevertheless, she can now express anger and is no longer completely depressed.

Finally, my experiences of working with these massively traumatized patients leads me to believe that the analyst's omnipotent wish to rescue and repair those whose lives have been so ravaged may also contain the guilt of the survivor and a need to mourn the reality of the Holocaust and those who have been lost. Once these unconscious needs have been worked through by the analyst, the intense countertransference that accepts the patient's projections so openly cannot be maintained. Natural defences against the acceptance of another's pain come into play and inevitably distance the analyst from the patient.

Nevertheless, the insights of psychoanalysis can help the survivor to accept that the murder of lost objects was not influenced by the wish fulfilments of childhood. Unconscious identification with the aggressor can be modified by working through, if the therapist can accept those painful roles of victim and aggressor in the transference. Mourning for the Holocaust and its victims is facilitated if the analyst accepts the sharing of suffering in the hope of alleviating despair. None the less, in my view the outcome depends upon the patient's individual life history before the camp and after. Both analyst and patient have to accept the limitation of insight in the face of massive traumatization.

Notes

1. I did not see then that this was an exciting acting-out in the transference of her unconscious sadomasochistic fantasies, in which my countertransference feelings of helplessness were an essential part of the drama.
2. At Dr Mengele's trial in Jerusalem, evidence showed that he frequently extracted healthy teeth as part of his experiments.
3. Six months later, Mrs C reported that she is no longer depressed but is able to express anger with her family when she feels unappreciated rather than continue the previous pattern of masochistic enslavement that had been forced upon her by Auschwitz. Her ability to acknowledge and express her own anger has enabled her to feel safer outside her home, and she is planning her first holiday in many years. But she is still haunted by Auschwitz.

THE IMPACT OF THE HOLOCAUST ON THE SECOND GENERATION*

My theme in this paper is the effect of the parents' Holocaust trauma on the second generation. In some families parents share the impact of the trauma with their children. In others disavowal of the Holocaust experience, in which the trauma is known but not known by the parents, leads to confusion in the children. This may be repeated in the analysis of the second generation, when that which is not known cannot be dealt with until the secret has been exposed.

Although warning of the impending disaster was brought to Great Britain by many European colleagues who came as refugees, none of them could possibly have anticipated the scale of genocide that took place in Europe in the twentieth century. The British Psycho-Analytical

* Presented at the 37th International Psychanalytical Congress, Buenos Aires, July 1991.

Society was enriched by the influx of these colleagues. Amongst them was Sigmund Freud, who was accompanied by his daughter Anna. Before them Melanie Klein, Paula Heimann and Karl Abraham's daughter had arrived from Berlin. Later, other members of the German Society – amongst them Barbara Lantos, Hilde Maas and Edyth Ludowyk – joined them. Ilse Hellman came from Vienna. Thus the European colleagues who joined the British Society could, from their own subjective experience, empathize with the Jews' terror and fear regarding the triumph of Adolf Hitler. They could be sympathetic listeners to refugees and survivors. Nevertheless, only two papers concerning the problems of survivor children were published by refugee analysts. Anna Freud reported on observations made by her staff on a group of children who had lived together in a concentration camp, and after being rescued were brought to England as a group (A. Freud, 1951). Despite the fact that several children were in analysis with members of the Hampstead Clinic staff, only one paper was published by Edyth Ludowyk Gyomroi (1963) describing the analysis of one of them. Now that the older generation have died, there is little interest in the second generation of analysts – to which I belong – in the problems of survivors and their children. It is as if the silence that shrouded the older generation of survivors and prevented them from telling their children about the past was reflected in the silence of the second generation of analysts who cannot *hear* what survivors and their children cannot *speak* openly. Thus mourning for the six million who died or for those members of the family who perished could not be worked through in analysis, since they remain secret figures from the parents' and patients' past.

The overwhelming trauma and tragedy of the Holocaust and the suffering of those European Jews who were caught in it, have affected my generation, since we were alive at that time. Many survivors who were liberated from the camps, or emerged from hiding to find their families destroyed, were impelled to abandon their countries of origin, where they had found no shelter, and face a new emigration. Many went to Israel, where the tragic reality of their past could be gradually accepted by fellow Jews, and their shame and loss of dignity could be worked through in an identification with a young and vigorous nation. Mourning for their losses could be shared by a whole population who participated in the Holocaust commemoration day, and erected museums, archives and memorials to the six million who had perished. The open acceptance by both patient and therapist of the reality of the Holocaust experience, and the empathy of Israeli analysts, helped others to live again. The analyst's sympathetic and open countertransference enables the patient to re-experience the trauma in the analytic space in order to gain access to the infantile conflicts and early emotions that preceded it, and gain relief.

Such an atmosphere did not exist in Great Britain, where many survivors sought refuge. No public recognition of their tragedy was shown; many remained hidden in the population, and were silent. Thus a state of mind which Freud (1925) described as 'blindness of the seeing eye in which one knows and does not know a thing at the same time' was not difficult to achieve for survivors, their children and the psychotherapeutic community to which they turned. Freud named this state of mind (a non-psychotic form of denial) *Verleugnung*, 'disavowal' in English. In 1939 he wrote of it as a half-measure in which the 'disavowal is always supplemented by an acknowledgement. Two contrary and independent attitudes result in a splitting of the ego.' Basch (1983) has suggested that disavowal, unlike psychiatric denial, obliterates only the significance of things, not their perception. An almost psychotic state may develop in the area between the splits, giving rise to an undercurrent of mythical and unreal states which give meaning to the patient's life. To my mind, this is the dilemma of survivors. Such a state of mind is eloquently described by Eli Wiesel: 'Had we started to speak we would have found it impossible. Having shed one tear we would have drowned the human heart. People refused to listen, to understand, to share. There was a division between us and them, between those who endured and those who read about it.'

In my clinical experience, disavowal hampers communication between survivors and their children. The survivor's child may be sensitive to the parent's secrets, which are never talked about, yet are sensed. These may give rise to intensely sexualized sadomasochistic fantasies which are acted out in masturbatory fantasies, or in adult relationships, or in the transference and countertransference of the analytic relationship. Alternatively, the children of survivors who love their parents may long to repair and rescue them from their pain and sadness by restoring their lost beloved objects. Thus they may unconsciously identify with the lost objects, or even become them at a cost to their own identity. Many such children may, without conscious knowledge of the secret, sense that they are replacements for those who were murdered in the Holocaust. Unconsciously, they may feel burdened by an ill-defined sense of obligation towards their parents, whose happiness depends upon them. They may accept or reject the task. Thus separation and individuation at the appropriate times in the life cycle may be difficult to achieve.

Working in analysis with survivors of the Holocaust has led me to believe that the completion of mourning, in which the lost objects are not forgotten but daily remembrance of them can be given up, is impeded by the guilt of the survivor. Many survivors live in a double reality into which new objects have been assimilated without replacing the old. For these survivors, replacing the murdered objects or forgetting them, unconsciously, produces a sense of guilt at not only murdering them in fantasy and burying them, but also surviving them. Many survivors whose families were murdered during the Holocaust longed to bring healthy children into a world no longer dominated by death, dehumanization, terror and sadism. The dilemma of the older survivor who has lost his or her first family, remarried, and had other children is particularly poignant. The first family is kept alive in his or her mind. The second family of children are replacements for the first one, since mourning and forgetting have not taken place. These parents are then unable to provide a foundation of security and safety in early object relationships for the second children. For example, a mother's experience in the Holocaust may have affected her capacity to empathize, and be emotionally available to her child. This is particularly so in the case of a woman who has lost children in the Holocaust. We know from women's dreams that a dead child is always somewhere in the mother's mind. In my experience second-generation children may be less affected if it is the father who has sustained the losses rather than the first caretaker, the mother, who can then provide a secure foundation for her baby.

However, many survivors have led energetic, successful lives since the Holocaust; their children do not necessarily show signs of trauma, and we do not hear much about them. The psychic development of children, and the outcome of the infantile neurosis, depends not only on their own psychic constitution but also on the maturational environment provided by their parents and the generations before them. It follows that parents who have suffered so much – not only in the concentration camps but also in difficult post-liberation conditions such as Displaced Persons' camps – may not only transmit depression and the guilt of the survivor, but also expect their children to vindicate their suffering (Levine, 1982). These children may be expected to fulfil their parents' interrupted hopes and dreams, as if they had no separate identity. Transmitted pathological parental identifications may also damage them (Barocas and Barocas, 1979). Thus grandparents, their lives, and the manner in which they died, as well as the fate of the parents' siblings, form a part of the child's early background if the working-through of mourning has not been achieved by the parents. Many remain silent.

By living through their children, the parents hoped to re-establish a family life that had been destroyed, and vicariously live through them parts of the life cycle of which they themselves had been deprived. Naturally, many of these children are over-valued and over-protected by their parents, whether the secret of the Holocaust is revealed or not. Many are expected to live in a state of perpetual happiness in order to make their parents happy. The normal vicissitudes of childlike pleasure, aggression and pain are frequently not acceptable to the parents. Thus the developmental growth of the pre-genital phases of life – love and hate for the same object, hostility and reparation, which eventually leads to the establishment of a whole object – is difficult to achieve. Ambivalence, in which the good aspects can be held as well as the bad, is not attained. In severe cases these children may grow into adults who have difficulty in recognizing and controlling their affects. They may resort to primitive defences, such as splitting and projection into others of their own intolerable emotions. Thus the child's self and object differentiation, and the normal development states of separation and individuation, are complicated by the parents' Holocaust experience, which may or may not be openly shared with their children. The trauma of the Holocaust is known and not known at the same time. It is my impression that problems have not arisen so strongly in children when the parents have openly talked about their lives.

Clinical experience leads me to believe that the Holocaust experience may remain as secret in the analytic space as in the family, and that the revelation of such unbearable material may be avoided by the collusion of both patient and analyst in a mutual state of disavowal. Here I would like to address the theme of what remains hidden in analysis, or is sometimes consciously known but not revealed to the analyst. Such material may be exposed and recovered to the patient's benefit if the analyst allows herself to *hear* in the patient's material that of which the patient is not consciously aware – namely, the impact of the Holocaust on her development. The price the analyst pays for attempting to face what is unbearable to the patient and her family may be an unbearable countertransference. The analyst risks the temporary breakdown of her own human understanding, and experiences in herself the negative empathy of some survivors' children towards their tragic parents. She may even have to experience in herself – and recognize – her own unaccustomed and shocking dehumanization of the patient, for dehumanization of the other is easily available to all human beings.

In turning to the clinical material which I have chosen to illustrate my theme, I would like to quote a passage from George Steiner: 'The black mystery of what happened in Europe is to me indivisible from my own identity. Precisely because I was not there.' None of the patients I describe 'was there'. All were born after the end of the

211

last War. An interesting paper by Nadine Fresco (Fresco, 1984) describes interviews with eight survivors' children. Many of the themes she describes – the silence in the family about the Holocaust, the children's fantasies, and the uncompleted task of mourning – were present in my patients, and had to be worked through in analysis. Two of my patients were children born to replace others who had perished. All of them were burdened by the imposs- ible duty of making up for their parents' irreparable losses. Thus some of them suffered from the guilt of the survivor, since they themselves were the living children who could never achieve the place in their parents' minds of the dead child, who remained an unchanging object of love. Or they suffered from an indefinable sense of being an impostor, a replacement for the dead child, as well as having an identity and a life of their own. Many felt guilty about their rage towards their parents, who did not recognize their separate identity, yet those parents had suffered so much.

Clinical Material

Mrs A consulted me in her late thirties because of her conflict about having a child, and her conscious awareness that the time available before her menopause was getting short. She was aware of a strong wish to conceive and bear a child in her present satisfying relationship, but she also felt a strong resistance to the idea. After the War her mother, who had been a vigorous member of the Parti- sans, talked openly about their heroic resistance to the Nazis, and was proud of it. Thus from her earliest years the Holocaust was part of family life. Her father had lost his first wife and four-year-old son, and was gloomy and depressed. He openly said that his 'real life' had been before the Holocaust, and the two children felt that he only half existed in the family. He said that things were right before the Holocaust, and nothing his living children could do would put them right again for him. The ghosts of the lost wife and child were always present, and he lived in a double reality, as many survivors do, for mourning them would feel to him as if he had killed them. This had affected his little girl's self-esteem, her sexual development and her fantasy life. However, in identification with her strong mother she had fought to achieve a successful professional life. Despite years of analysis in her own country, the impact of the Holocaust had never been touched upon or understood. In the consultation it emerged that she had never been sure of her female sexual identity, and this had complicated her wish for a child. In her fantasy she had always been the replacement child for the dead little blond boy who had made her father happy. In this way, real life would be restored and her father would be made happy again in the present. She went on to reveal a conscious fantasy that had existed from her early childhood: that her father would die if she had a child. Gradually we understood that if she allowed herself to conceive a child and confirm her own female sexual identity, the boy part of her would have to die, and part of her father would have to die again. She could not allow this, since in fantasy she would be the Nazi who murdered the little boy ghost that she had kept alive in herself for her father's sake. Mrs A was relieved that this hidden material had been found in the analytic space of the consultation. Since she did not live in England, we could not continue with an analysis.

My second patient, Miss J, appeared to have had a fairly happy childhood. Her father had emigrated from Eastern Europe to America before the War, and her mother had been born there. Their marriage was tranquil, but at times her father was withdrawn. At puberty Miss J showed considerable disturbance, and was helped by a long analysis in which oedipal and pre-oedipal material was worked through. Her previous analyst referred her to me because she was coming to London. She was a stocky girl, with a heavy body and an expressionless face. I was astonished to hear that she had come to England to train as a ballet dancer. It seemed to me that there was some distortion of reality in her perception of herself, and I was not surprised to learn that she was failing in her training. Nevertheless, she persevered single-mindedly. As the therapeutic alliance developed, Miss J trusted me enough to tell me about some of her strange actions. In particular, although she was living in a student hostel where adequate meals were provided, she crept downstairs every night after lights out to an outside yard where the dustbins were kept. She rummaged through them for scraps of food, salvaging half-eaten pieces of bread and other bits which she ate equally stealthily hidden in the dark. This behaviour was so bizarre that I felt it was a psychotic acting-out, and that she was much more ill than I had realized. As the sessions proceeded I began to be aware that in my own mind I was talking not only with Miss J, but also with someone else who occupied her body and her mind.

This was a projection on to me of Miss J's own state of mind. I was impelled to ask her if she had a second name. She replied that it was Ilse and that she was named after a young aunt, her father's sister, who had perished in a concentration camp. Her aunt was training to be a ballet dancer and had died when she was nineteen, the age that Miss J was when she came to Europe to do her training. Her mother had told her this, but her father had never mentioned his sister or his mother, who had both met the fate that he had escaped by emigration.

214

We then understood together that Miss J was living in a double reality – that of her own life as it was, but also in her fantasy the life that Ilse had lived in the camp. It appeared that her reality-testing had become as distorted as I had noted in her body image. The bizarre symptomatology disappeared after the unconscious fantasy had become conscious, and could be worked through. I am glad to say that she gave up her unsuccessful attempt to become a ballet dancer. What had appeared to be psychotic was a localized failure to appreciate the difference between reality and fantasy.

Through what I learned from my countertransference, I wonder whether Miss J's failure to appreciate the difference between reality and fantasy could in part have been due to her father's repressed mourning for the sister he never spoke of. It was as if in the countertransference I, like him, saw his nineteen-year-old daughter returning to Europe both as herself, and in fantasy as nineteen-year-old Ilse. I saw the same phenomenon in the case of a girl whose older sister had been killed in the Holocaust long before she was born.

Working with Miss J drew my attention to the impact that returning to Europe can have on some children whose parents emigrated to other countries. I found the same pattern with several other patients whose parents or grandparents had experienced the Holocaust. Their return to Europe seemed to bring to light aspects of their identity that had previously been hidden. As Blum has pointed out, early identification is based upon a process of internal selection and internalization, and is partly influenced by environmental cues (Blum, 1986). The identifications of these chidren seem to have been influenced by the environment in which their parents lived when they were very young, at a time when their parents had only recently been released. They were still in a state of trauma from the human losses they had sustained. Many were depressed and unable to provide their child with a safe early object relationship. The good-enough parenting necessary for a healthy process of internalization and identification was simply not available. When they later made a successful life elsewhere they provided their children with a different maturational environment, and these children were able to internalize a stronger sense of identity. In my experience, however, the archaic object representations remain hidden beneath these superimposed and more efficient ego processes, and reappear in the form of ego weaknesses or developmental arrests of identity to which the patient may be fixated.

The emotional scars of the Holocaust affect not only the children of the victims and their analysts but also the children of the oppressors and their analysts. Eckstaedt (1986) has emphasized the importance of empathizing with the reality of the trauma afflicting the children of the oppressors. As I have described elsewhere (Pines, 1986), working with victims of the Holocaust and the children of survivors has convinced me of the same view. Eike Hinze (1986) described the influence of real historical events on a German patient's life. Eckstaedt (1986) writes about the effect on the personality structure of two second-generation young German men of their fathers' strong belief in the Nazi Third Reich. My own experience of working with a non-Jewish German patient of my own generation impressed me with the strength of the inhibition and silence that reigns in Germany concerning the events of the Third Reich, and the difficulty that some analysts experience in *hearing* the patients' communications on such an unbearable topic.

*

Mrs D, a German, consulted me during a short but intensive time of psychoanalytic treatment. Characteristically, she did not approach me directly but asked a colleague of mine to find out whether I would see her. She had hidden behind someone else, and thus the central theme of silence and hiding was acted out with me before I actually met her. Consciously, Mrs D had reached the menopause without bearing a child, and felt sad about it. She had read various published papers of mine and felt I could help her to mourn the fertile time of her life which had now passed. We arranged that she would come to London and we would meet twice a day for three weeks. Initially I felt some reluctance to engage with this patient, a woman who shared the historical past of my own life, but as a child of persecutors rather than a grandchild of victims, as I myself was. I wondered how the intense aspects of transference and countertransference would be affected by our previous histories and lives.

Mrs D was a tall, heavy woman with a very musical voice. She had always taken part in amateur musical performances, and worked successfully as a music therapist with extremely disturbed children. She felt that she was always too late for everything and now, when she could no longer become pregnant, was the time at which she longed for children. Since we were meeting twice a day, the therapeutic alliance developed rapidly and Mrs D's story unfolded.

She had been born in a small farming village in North Germany, where her family had lived for several generations. Both her father and her paternal grandmother were delighted by the child's birth, but her mother, who had been anorexic, was more ambivalent. In fact Mrs D learnt much later that her mother had denied her pregnancy and made no preparations for her birth. However, for her grandmother she was a replacement child – her own daughter had died when she was three. Thus father and paternal grandmother provided her with consistent love at the beginning of her life, compensating for the fact that her mother often went into hospital for treatment of her anorexia. Her father was drafted into the German army and sent to Russia when she was one-and-a-half years old. Her paternal grandmother and her mother remained on the family farm. All the men in the village served in an SS unit, but her father asked to be transferred to an ordinary army unit. Mrs D was always writing him letters through her grandmother, and was delighted by the drawings he sent her in reply. He was always in her mind – this was doubtless encouraged by his mother, although her own mother remained cold and remote. When she was three her father was posted to a local town, and she lived with him for some months until he was sent to Russia. Mrs D was always told how happy he was in Russia, and how good the Russians had been to him. She repeated this with such fervour, like a naive child, that I was astonished, since history seemed to have reported otherwise – thus I too knew but did not know.

Her grandmother would not shop at stores confiscated from Jews, and she, her mother and her paternal grandfather were kind to the *Fremdarbeiter*, slave foreign workers, and the prisoners of war who were sent to work on the farm. Her mother warned her that she must not tell the rest of the village that the prisoners ate at the table with them and were well treated, or they themselves might be punished. She did not tell anyone, nor did she speak of the cruel ritual that happened every day between her mother and herself. At eleven o'clock, when everyone was working in the fields, her mother drew the curtains and silently beat her. The child defied her and never cried out, but bore the suffering silently.

When Mrs D was knocked down by a car, she had a

severe head injury and was taken to hospital. There her wounds were sutured without an anaesthetic and her mother did nothing; she did not hold her and try to comfort her while she was screaming with fear and pain. In my view this was the beginning of Mrs D's identification with suffering people who could not escape from cruelty. She had witnessed animals being cruelly slaughtered in the village, although the war that was raging elsewhere did not affect the small, isolated community. The prisoners of war were kind to her and made her toys, and she made friends with the little daughter of a Polish woman who had volunteered to work in Germany. Frequently they sat together on the doorstep and cried about their missing daddies.

I had been wondering throughout this time not only where the theme of childlessness had disappeared to, but also who I was in the transference. It seemed to me that I must represent the *Fremdarbeiter*, the slave worker or the child with whom she had shared sorrow. It was as if in the analytic space we were two little girls who both knew and did not know. Following this interpretation Mrs D astonished me by revealing a secret that had been consciously concealed from me so far. She had first seen me when I spoke at a large conference in Germany and, without my knowledge, had followed me silently ever since – for about fifteen years. She did not come to any more conferences, but found out through her friends where I was going to be, and persuaded them to bring my papers to her. Thus she acted out being the child who observed everything, knew everything, but remained silent. The person she observed was totally unaware of what was happening.

From this point on Mrs D began to reveal other secrets of her childhood. She had felt very guilty about her open death wishes towards her mother. When her father returned from Russia she told him of her mother's cruelty to her. He stopped his wife's attacks and told Mrs D that he had thought seriously about divorcing her mother, but had decided to stay for his daughter's sake. From that time onwards she slept between her parents in their matrimonial bed. In this way her father punished his wife by frustrating her, excited his young daughter, and satisfied neither. He had frightening nightmares and frequently his tormented wife wandered around the house at night, and Mrs D got up to console her. So she became mother to her own mother. Despite her parents' opposition she did brilliantly at university, returning home every vacation to sleep between her parents again. Intellectually she was separate, but the incestuous feelings between her father and herself always drew her back to her home. Later Mrs D identified her angry and hurt father in her own adult life. Despite the fact that she had married a distinguished man who loved her, she openly and frequently had lovers, thus having two men in her bed and reversing her childhood situation by frustrating her husband. In this way her father's serious confusion in his identity as a father and his identity as a husband was repeated by Mrs D. She always dressed like a little girl.

Again Mrs D returned to the theme of how good her family had been to the prisoners, and how they had all returned after the War to thank them. She herself had been to stay with one of them in France. Gradually she began to talk about the cruelty of other villagers, not only in slaughtering animals but also in maltreating the prisoners. Mrs D went on to tell me that she had been very moved by the film of the Holocaust that was shown in Germany, which she had seen when she was in her first analysis, but she had not been able to share the experience with her German analyst. Silence by both analyst and patient, who shared a common past, did not allow for

220

shared pain, mourning, shame and guilt. I asked her whether she had brought these subjects to her analysis in Germany. She said that she had mentioned them, but the analyst did not take it up; it was therefore both known and not known.

It seemed to me that something was being enacted rather than talked about. I felt that repeated in the transference to the German analyst were the ambivalent childhood feelings she had experienced towards her severe and sadistic mother before her father came back: a mixture of defiance, rage and fear of retaliation, with no room for mutual sharing of pain. Had the Polish woman, the *Fremdarbeiterin*, secretly been someone she could turn to for mothering and for consolation? Had she always secretly been in her mind, as I had been until she needed me? Mrs D accepted my interpretation and said sadly that the woman and her daughter had been sent away to a factory, and suddenly screamed with horror that it had been Auschwitz. A stunned silence filled the room, and neither of us could speak. So the child's secret knowledge of Auschwitz was revealed, and the split of affect experienced in the session. She could now openly mourn for her beloved dead, as I could mourn for mine. We thus understood that behind the difficulty of mourning for childlessness lay the secret uncompleted mourning for the victims she had loved.

Conclusion

The four second-generation patients I have discussed in this paper are affected by their parents' Holocaust experiences, despite the fact that none of the parents had actually been a survivor from a concentration camp. Winnicott once wrote that there is 'no such a thing as a baby' (Winnicott, 1965): he meant that where one finds an infant, one finds maternal care. Thus the patients in analysis with me brought into the analytic space not only their own psychopathology but also that of their mothers and fathers. The child's ego development and integration depended not only on the mother herself, but also on her own Holocaust history and her mastery of it. The secret brought into the analytic space was the aspect of the patient's identity that the patient herself had not known.

Mrs A's mother fought heroically with the Jewish Partisans. Thus she had been able to use her aggression to resist dehumanization, and to avenge the lives of those who had been murdered. She appeared adequately to have mourned the loss of her old world, and to have enjoyed making a new and interesting world for herself and her family. It was the shadow of her murdered half-brother that fell across Mrs A's gender and sexual identity, although she could identify with a strong mother in the rest of her life. Miss J's mother was born in America and was unaffected by the Holocaust. Although Miss J had other problems which needed further analysis, the impact of the Holocaust became evident on her first trip to Europe, as if it were a drama that had never been verbalized in the family. The symptom disappeared after it had been recognized and worked through.

Mrs D, the German patient, had a secret in her life which had never been divulged in her previous analysis, and needed to be heard. Having seen and heard me many years earlier in Germany she, too, on the strength of a mild physical resemblance, needed to share with me the sadness and pain of the loss of the Polish mother and daughter, whom she had always hoped would come back. Accepting their terrible fate, and naming it Auschwitz, shows that she had both known and not known. She could then mourn them and resume life. For until the trauma is faced, named, known and shared, it lies deep inside us all, and cannot be exorcized.

If psychic change is to be effected in psychoanalysis, the traumatic factors in the patient's life must enter the psychoanalytic space in the patient's own way and within the patient's omnipotence (Winnicott, 1975). In my view the analyst, when treating these traumatized patients, must use reliability and empathy in order not only to hear what the patient says but also to hear and understand what has not been verbally expressed so far. In this way the adult in the patient can succeed in mastering what the child could not master, since the parents could not help. Thus the trauma of the Holocaust can to some extent be exposed and worked through in analysis. Mourning for what has been lost can be expressed, and the secret identity of the patients with those who have died can be laid to rest. The process of separation and individuation can develop from where it had once been impeded. Mrs A, Miss J and Mrs D were relieved by psychoanalysis.

Finally, in writing a paper about the impact of the Holocaust on the second generation, I have come to realize that here, more than in any other paper I have previously written, I have been engaged not only in the rediscovery of my patients' Holocaust history and its impact on their lives, but also – as for all analysts of my generation – in the rediscovery of my own. Thus I too am deeply affected by the guilt of the survivor. The sense of psychic continuity that is important to us all was brutally broken in my patients' lives, but also to some degree in my own. It is as though an unquiet grave for our murdered forebears, a hole in family tradition as a result of twentieth-century European history, cannot be repaired by the normal process of mourning. The meaning of disavowal, as defined by Basch, is a defence against the dangers of external reality and extreme trauma. The Holocaust was an unthinkable experience until it happened in reality. The true meaning of what was accurately perceived was banned from emerging into consciousness in both patient and therapist, by mutual collusion.

I was astonished to find that although I thought I had some notes on the patients I have described in this paper, they were not there. What I write about is therefore reconstructed from memories, more vivid than my memories about most patients, so that I also both know and do not know. The intense projections I encountered from these patients frequently aroused overwhelming impulses in me to avoid the topic, to stop thinking and remembering, and to distract myself. It was as though the identification with the aggressor so frequently encountered in survivor parents, and so frequently transmitted to the next generation, forced me into attempting to escape from the overwhelming world of torture and sadism they had endured, and unconsciously inflicted on their children. I could understand why the daughters of a survivor patient of mine constantly sought to be reborn in fantasy, in a rebirthing ceremony, and made disastrous marriages to non-Jews – thus unconsciously attempting to save their non-Jewish children from the fate of their parents' Jewish families that had been murdered. For they knew, from their parents' suffering, that the price we paid for a Jewish identity also comprises what we know and cannot bear, that we belong to a community with a long history of persecution and martyrdom.

The Holocaust in the twentieth century confirmed the reality of that risk. If, as analysts, we work with children of survivors, we must also accept the strong emotions projected by the patient when the Holocaust silence is broken and the trauma is exposed. We must have the strength to bear the unbearable countertransference that mirrors what is unbearable and secret in every human being – the impact of the fragility of civilization in patient and analyst alike, which tries to defend against a deeper evil: man's inhumanity to man.

BIBLIOGRAPHY

Abbreviations

Annual Psychoanal.	*The Annual of Psycho-Analysis*
Int. J. Psycho-Anal.	*International Journal of Psycho-Analysis*
Int. Rev. Psycho-Anal.	*International Review of Psycho-Analysis*
J. Amer. Psychoanal. Assn.	*Journal of the American Psychoanalytic Association*
Psychoanal. Quart.	*Psychoanalytic Quarterly*
Psychoanal. Study Child	*Psychoanalytic Study of the Child*

Anthony, E. J. and **Benedek, T.** (1970) *Parenthood: Its Psychology and Psychopathology*. Boston, MA: Little, Brown.

Balint, E. (1973) 'Technical problems found in the analysis of a woman by a woman analyst'. *Int. J. Psycho-Anal.* 54: 195–201.

Balint, M. (1950) 'Changing therapeutical aims and techniques in psycho-analysis'. *Int. J. Psycho-Anal.* 31: 117–24.
—— (1952) 'On love and hate'. *Int. J. Psycho-Anal.* 54: 195–201.
—— (1968) *The Basic Fault*. London: Tavistock.

Barocas, H. and **Barocas, C.** (1979) 'Wounds of the fathers: the next generation of Holocaust victims'. *Int. Rev. Psycho-Anal.* 3: 331–41.

Basch, M. (1983) 'The Perception of Reality and the Disavowal of Meaning', in *Annual Psychoanal.* 11: 125–54.

Benedek, T. (1950) 'Climacterium: a developmental phase'. *Psychoanal. Quart.* 19: 1–27.
—— (1959) 'Parenthood as a developmental phase'. *J. Amer. Psychoanal Assn* 7: 389–417.

Bibring, G. L., Dwyer, T. F., Huntington, D. S. and **Valenstein,**

A. F. (1961) 'A study of the psychological processes in pregnancy and of the earliest mother–child relationship'. *Psychoanal. Study Child.* 16: 9–72.

Bick, E. (1968) 'The experience of the skin in early object-relations'. *Int. J. Psycho-Anal.* 49: 484–6.

Blum, H. (1976) 'Masochism, the ego ideal and the psychology of women'. *J. Amer. Psychoanal. Assn* 24 (suppl.): 157–91.
—— (1986) 'On identification and its vicissitudes'. *Int. J. Psycho-Anal.* 67: 267.

Caplan, G. (1959) *Concepts of Mental Health and Consultation.* Washington, DC: US Children's Bureau.
—— (1961) *An Approach to Community Mental Health.* London: Tavistock.

Deutsch, H. (1944) *The Psychology of Women.* New York: Grune & Stratton.
—— (1945) 'Epilogue: the climacterium', in *The Psychology of Women,* 2. New York: Grune & Stratton.

Eckstaedt, A. (1986) 'Two complementary cases of identification'. *Int. J. Psycho-Anal.* 67: 317.

Erikson, E. H. (1959) *Identity and the Life Cycle. Issues, Monogr 1.* New York: International Universities Press.

Fresco, N. (1984) 'Remembering the unknown'. *Int. Rev. Psycho-Anal.* 11: 417.

Freud, A. (1967) 'Comments on trauma', in S. Furst (ed.), *Psychic Trauma.* New York: Basic Books, pp. 235–45.
—— and **Dann, S.** (1951) 'An experiment in group upbringing'. *Psychoanal. Study Child* 6: 127–68; 22: 126.

Freud, S. (1905) 'Fragment of an analysis of a case of hysteria. Postscript', in James Strachey (ed.), *The Standard Edition of the Complete Psychological Works of Sigmund Freud,* 24 vols. London: Hogarth, 1953–73, vol. 7.
—— (1909) 'Analysis of a phobia in a five-year-old boy'. *S.E.* 3: 148.
—— (1912) 'The dynamics of transference'. *S.E.* 12: 97–108.

—— (1916–17) 'The archaic features and infantilism of dreams'. *S.E.* 15: 202.

—— (1925) 'Negation'. *S.E.* 19: 235.

—— (1935) *An Autobiographical Study. S.E.* 20.

—— (1939) *Complemental Series, S.E.* 23: 73.

Gampel, Y. (1982) 'A metapsychological assessment based on an analysis of a survivor's child', in *Generations of the Holocaust.* New York: Basic Books.

Greenacre, P. (1954) 'The role of transference'. *J. Amer. Psychoanal. Assn* 2: 671–84.

Greenson, R. (1965) 'The working alliance and the transference neurosis'. *Psychoanal. Quart.* 34: 155–81.

Grubrich-Simitis, I. (1984) 'From concretization to metaphor'. *Psychoanal. Study Child* 39: 301–19.

Gyomroi, E. L. (1963) 'The analysis of a young concentration camp victim'. *Psychoanal. Study Child* 18: 484–510.

Heimann, P. (1950) 'On counter-transference'. *Int. J. Psycho-Anal.* 31: 81–4.

—— (1956) 'Dynamics of transference interpretation'. *Int. J. Psycho-Anal.* 37: 303–10.

Hinze, E. (1986) 'The influence of historical events on psychoanalysis'. *Int. J. Psycho-Anal.* 67, 4, 459.

Hoffer, W. (1956) 'Transference and transference neuroses'. *Int. J. Psycho-Anal.* 37: 377–9.

James, M. (1978) 'Psychosomatic symptoms as failed defence'. Unpublished paper presented at the English Speaking Conference.

Joseph, B. (1975) 'The patient who is difficult to reach', in P. Giovacchini (ed.), *Tactics and Techniques in Psychoanalytic Therapy*, vol. 2. New York: Aronson.

Kestenberg, J. (1974) 'Notes on parenthood as a developmental phase'. *J. Amer. Psychoanal. Assn* 23: 154–65. (Panel on parenthood, reported by H. Parens.)

—— (1982) 'A metapsychological assessment based on analysis of a survivor's child', in M. Bergmann and M. Jocovy (eds), *Generations of the Holocaust*. New York: Basic Books.

Khan, M. M. R. (1963) 'The concept of cumulative trauma'. *Psychoanal. Study Child* 18.
—— (1974) 'La rancune de l'hystérique'. *Nouvelle Revue Psychoanalytique* 10: 151–8.
—— (1974) *The Privacy of the Self*. London: Hogarth.

King, P. B. (1978) 'Affective response of the analyst to the patient's communication'. *Int. J. Psycho-Anal.* 59: 329–34.

Kogan, I. (1990) 'Working through the vicissitudes of trauma in the psychoanalysis of Holocaust survivors' offspring'. *Psyche* 6: 533–45.

Kohut, H. (1959) 'Introspection, empathy, and psychoanalysis'. *J. Amer. Psychoanal. Assn* 7: 459–83.

Krystal, H. (ed.) (1968) *Massive Psychic Trauma*. New York: International, Universities Press.
—— (1971) 'Trauma', in H. Krystal and W. G. Niederland (eds), *Psychic Traumatization*. Boston, MA: Little, Brown.
—— (1974) 'The genetic development of affects and affect regression'. *Annual Psychoanal.* 2: 98–126.
—— (1975) 'Affect tolerance'. *Annual Psychoanal.* 3: 179–219.
—— (1977) 'Aspects of affect theory'. *Bulletin of the Menninger Clinic* 41: 1–26.
—— and Niederland, W. G. (1968) 'Clinical observations of the survivor syndrome', in H. Krystal (ed.), *Massive Psychic Trauma*.

Laufer, M. and **Laufer, E.** (1984) *Adolescent Developmental Breakdown*. New Haven, CT: Yale University Press.

Lax, R. (1982) 'The expectable depressive climacteric reaction'. *Bulletin of the Menninger Clinic* 46: 151–67.

Leboyer, F. (1974) *A Child is Born* (film).

Levine, B. (1982) 'Children of survivors of the Holocaust'. *Psychoanal. Quart.* 51: 70.

Lifton, R. J. (1967) *Death in Life: Survivors of Hiroshima.* New York: Random House.

Limentani, A. (1977) 'Affects and the psychoanalytic situation'. *Int. J. Psycho-Anal.* 58: 171–82.

Mahler, M. (1975) *The Psychological Birth of the Human Infant.* London: Hutchinson.

Marty, P. and **M'Uzan, M. de** (1963) 'La "pensée opératoire"'. *Revue Française Psychoanalytique* 27: 1345–56.

McDougall, J. (1972) 'Primal scene and sexual perversion'. *Int. J. Psycho-Anal.* 53: 371–84.
—— (1974) 'The psychosoma and the psychoanalytic process'. *Int. Rev. Psycho-Anal.* 1: 437–59.

Mehra, B. and **Pines, D.** (1972) 'Study of promiscuous girls under the auspices of the Centre for Adolescent Research' (unpublished).

Moses, R. (1984) 'An Israeli psychoanalyst looks back in 1983', in *Psychoanalytic Reflections on the Holocaust.* Israel: Ktav.

Niederland, W. G. (1961) 'The problem of the survivor'. *Journal of Hillside Hospital* 10: 233–47.

Notman, M. (1982) 'The midlife years and after'. *Journal of Geriatric Psychiatry* 15: 173–91.

Pines, D. (1972) 'Pregnancy and motherhood: interaction between fantasy and reality'. *British Journal of Medical Psychiatry* 45: 333–43.
—— (1980) 'Skin communication: early skin disorders and their effect on transference and countertransference'. *Int. J. Psycho-Anal.* 61: 315–23.
—— (1982) 'The relevance of early psychic development to pregnancy and abortion'. *Int. J. Psycho-Anal.* 63: 311–19.
—— (1986) 'Working with Women Survivors of the Holocaust: Affective Experiences in Transference and Countertransference'. *Int. J. Psycho-Anal.* 67: 295–306.

Rapoport, R. (1963) 'Normal crises: family structure and mental health'. *Family Process* 2: 68–80.

Stoller, R. J. (1968) *Sex and Gender*. London: Hogarth.

Winnicott, D. W. (1965) 'Ego distortion in terms of true and false self', in *The Maturational Processes and the Facilitating Environment*. London: Hogarth.
—— (1975) 'Primary maternal pre-occupation', in *Through Paediatrics to Psychoanalysis*. London: Hogarth.

GLOSSARY

Acting-Out: Action in which the subject in the grip of her unconscious wishes and fantasies relives these in the present with a sensation of immediacy which is heightened by her refusal to recognise their source and their repetitive character.

Affect: Term which connotes any affective state, whether painful or pleasant, whether vague or well-defined, and whether it is manifested in the form of a massive discharge or in the form of a general mood. The affect is the qualitative expression of the quantity of instinctual energy and of its fluctuations.

Aphanasis: Term introduced by Ernest Jones to describe the ultimate dread of losing all sexual desire and capacity for pleasure.

Cathect: Term invented by Freud's English translators to translate the German term *besetzung*, which Freud used to describe the quantity of energy attaching to any object-representation or mental structure.

Concretism: Term which denotes the absence of metaphor in a patient's narrative where fantasy and thought are not available.

Counter-transference: The whole of the analyst's unconscious reactions to the individual analysand, especially to the analysand's own transference.

Ego-Ideal: An agency of the personality resulting from the coming together of narcissism and identification with the parents, with their substitutes or with collective ideals. As a distinct agency, the ego-ideal constitutes a model to which the subject attempts to conform.

Libido: Energy underlying the transformations of the sexual

232

instinct with respect to its object, with respect to its aim, and with respect to the source of sexual excitation.

Object: Psychoanalysis considers the notion of object from three main points of view: the thing towards which action or desire is directed, that which the subject requires in order to achieve instinctual satisfaction, or that to which the subject relates herself.

Object-relationship: Term designating the subject's mode of relation to her world. An object-relationship may be either to an external or to an internal object.

Whole Object: A whole object is a person whom the subject recognises as such and as having similar rights, feelings and needs as herself.

Oedipal: Term describing a group of largely unconscious ideas and feelings centred on the wish to possess the parent of the opposite sex and to eliminate the parent of the same sex.

Pre-oedipal: Qualifies the period of psychosexual development preceding the formation of the oedipus complex or three persons stage. During this period attachment to the mother predominates in both sexes.

Pre-genital: Qualifies those phases of infantile libidinal development which precede the genital phase and the impulses and fantasies derived therefrom.

Primal scene: Scene of sexual intercourse between the parents which the child observes, or infers on the basis of certain indications, and fantasies. It is generally interpreted by the child as an act of violence on the part of the father.

Primigravida: A woman who is expecting her first child.

Projection: Operation whereby qualities, feelings, wishes or even 'objects' which the subject refuses to recognise or rejects in herself, are expelled from the self and located in another person or thing.

Reparation: Mechanism whereby the subject seeks to repair the effects her destructive fantasies have had on her love-object.

Somatic: Term which focuses on the subject's body response.

Splitting: Term which denotes the coexistence at the heart of the ego of two psychical attitudes towards external reality insofar as this stands in the way of an instinctual demand.

Transference: The process by which a patient displaces onto her analyst feelings, ideas, etc. which derive from previous figures in her life.

Working-through: Process by means of which analysis implants and overcomes the resistances to which it has given rise. Working-through is taken to be a sort of psychical work which allows the patient to accept certain repressed elements and to free herself from the grip of mechanisms of repetition.

INDEX

Abandonment, fear of, 1
Abortion, 5, 116–133; as
  communication, 5; and early
  psychic development,
  97–115; Holocaust survivor
  (clinical example), 121–122;
  and maturational
  environment (clinical
  example), 103–114; and
  pathological mourning, 64;
  as relief, 119; and retarded
  emotional development
  (clinical example), 125–132
Abraham, H., 3–4, 206
Abraham, K., 3, 206
Acting-out, vs. thinking, 6
Adhesive identification, 10
Adolescence: amenorrhoeia in,
  4; body image in, 84;
  changes in, importance of, 4,
  29; in concentration camp,
  182; conflicts of, in adult,
  27; developmental function
  of, 80; motherhood in, 78–96
  [pathological response to,
  82]; physical maturation in,
  135; pregnancy in, 70–71,
  78–96 [clinical example,
  70–71; poor self-image in,
  84–89]; promiscuity in,

42–58, 69–76, 86, 90–91,
  103 [clinical example,
  42–58]; separation-
  individuation in, 83, 118;
  use of body in, 69
Adoption, 134
Aggression, 5, 42–58;
  primitive, infantile, 13; and
  promiscuity in adolescence,
  42–58
Aggressor, identification with,
  187, 204
Ambivalence: maternal, 121,
  133; in parent-child
  relationships, 120
Amenorrhoeia, in adolescence,
  4
Analysis: communication in,
  4–5; as holding
  environment, 202;
  termination of, 132
Analyst: benevolence of, 6;
  compassion of, 6–7; as
  container of patient's
  feelings, 30; detachment of,
  197; empathy of, 40, 201,
  223; as father, 45; frailty of,
  denial of by patient, 18;
  identification of, 40;
  irritation of, 20, 24; as

235

Also of interest

THE PSYCHOANALYSIS OF CHILDREN
Melanie Klein

The Psychoanalysis of Children, first published in 1932, is a classic in its subject, and revolutionised child analysis. Melanie Klein had already proved, by the special technique she devised, that she was a pioneer in that branch of analysis. She made possible the extension of psychoanalysis to the field of early childhood, and in this way not only made the treatment of young children possible but also threw new light on psychological development in childhood and on the roots of adult neuroses and psychoses. *The Psychoanalysis of Children* describes both the theory and practice of her methods, and includes a preface, written for the third edition, in which she outlines the development of her thinking in relation to certain essential hypotheses.

Also by Melanie Klein

LOVE, GUILT AND REPARATION
and other works 1921–1945

The pre-eminent contribution of Melanie Klein's writings
has been crucial both to theoretical work and to clinical
practice. *Love, Guilt and Reparation* shows the growth of
Melanie Klein's work and ideas between 1921 and 1945.
The earlier papers reveal her intense preoccupation with
the impact of infant anxieties upon child development. She
traces these influences on criminality and childhood
psychosis, symbol formation and intellectual inhibition
and the early development of conscience. the later papers
on the psychogenesis of manic depressive states are a
major contribution to the understanding of infant
development during the second half-year of life. She
presents her conceptualisation of the central anxieties,
defences and development in what she came to call the
depressive position. In the final paper on the Oedipus
complex, Klein develops her theories of the earliest infant
stages of development, extending Freud's analysis of the
Oedipus complex and laying a basis for her own
subsequent conceptualising of the paranoid-schizoid
position in the first six months of life. The volume also
contains a foreword by Dr Hanna Segal and explanatory
notes by the Editorial Board of the Melanie Klein Trust.

Virago also publish *Narrative of a Child Analysis: The conduct
of the psychoanalysis of children as seen in the treatment of a
ten-year-old boy* and *Envy and Gratitude and other works
1946–1963*.

THE BONDS OF LOVE
Psychoanalysis, feminism and the problem of domination
Jessica Benjamin

'*The Bonds of Love* gives us Benjamin at her best, and psychoanalytic social theory at its best, as she demonstrates brilliantly the complex intertwining of familial, gender and social domination'
– *Nancy Chodorow*

Why do people submit to authority and even derive pleasure from the power others have over them? What is the appeal of domination and submission, and why are they so prevalent in erotic life? Why is it so difficult for men and women to meet as equals? Why indeed do they continue to recapitulate the positions of master and slave?

Jessica Benjamin makes use of her feminist reinterpretations of psychoanalytic theory to consider anew the problem of domination, of individual development, gender difference and authority. Domination is revealed as a complex psychological process which ensnares both parties in bonds of complicity, and one which underlies our family life, social institutions and especially sexual relationships, in spite of our conscious commitment to equality and freedom. In her questioning of gender polarities in which woman is object to the male subject she argues for a change which she describes as both 'modest and utopian' – in disentangling the bonds of love, we seek a mutual recognition of equal subjects which would lead to both personal and social transformation.

THE HANDS OF THE LIVING GOD
An Account of a Psychoanalytic Treatment
Marion Milner

'Marion Milner uses her fine intellect and her special reflective capacity and her modest certainty to give us a unique presentation of a treatment of great length and complexity . . . It rings true in every detail'
– D.W. Winnicott

This remarkable book, first published in 1969, is the detailed account of a case study of someone too divided within herself. In the treatment, lasting over twenty years, 'Susan' suddenly and spontaneously discovered the capacity to do doodle drawings. It was partly for this reason and also in order to clarify, both for herself and for others, what she was learning from her patients that Marion Milner wrote the book. But the ultimate stimulus came from the drawings themselves, with their deep unconscious perception of the nature of the battle between sanity and madness. Over 150 of 'Susan's' drawings have been reproduced, and it is these which, closely linked with Marion Milner's sensitive and lucid record of the therapeutic encounter, give the book its unique and compelling interest.